MEDITERRANEAN DIET

The Mediterranean Diet Cookbook for Beginners with Pictures : Easy and Delicious Recipes for Healthy Living / 21-Day Meal Plan to Lose Weight

Sadie Garcia

CONTENTS

INTRODUCTION
5

CHAPTER 1
BREAKFAST RECIPES
8

CHAPTER 2
LUNCH RECIPES
21

CHAPTER 3
DINNER RECIPES
36

CHAPTER 4
SALAD RECIPES
48

CHAPTER 5
SOUP RECIPES
57

CHAPTER 6
DESSERT RECIPE
63

CHAPTER 7
SMOOTHIE RECIPES
69

CHAPTER 8
21-DAY MEAL PLAN
73

© Copyright by Sadie Garcia 2023 - All rights reserved.

ISBN: 9798399409443

The content contained within this book may not be reproduced, duplicated or transmitted without direct written permission from the author or the publisher.
Under no circumstances will any blame or legal responsibility be held against the publisher, or author, for any damages, reparation, or monetary loss due to the information contained within this book
Either directly or indirectly. You are responsible for your own choices, actions, and results.

Legal Notice:
This book is copyright protected. This book is only for personal use. You cannot amend, distribute, sell, use, quote or paraphrase any part, or the content within this book, without the consent of the author or publisher.

Disclaimer Notice:
Please note the information contained within this document is for educational and entertainment purposes only. All effort has been executed to present accurate, up to date, and reliable, complete information. No warranties of any kind are declared or implied. Readers acknowledge that the author is not engaging in the rendering of legal, financial, medical or professional advice. The content within this book has been derived from various sources. Please consult a licensed professional before attempting any techniques outlined in this book.
By reading this document, the reader agrees that under no circumstances is the author responsible for any losses, direct or indirect, which are incurred as a result of the use of the information contained within this document, including, but not limited to, — errors, omissions, or inaccuracies.

Leave a review about our book:
As an independent author with a small marketing budget, reviews are my livelihood on this platform. If you enjoyed this book, I'd really appreciate it, if you left your honest feedback. You can do so by clicking review button.

I love hearing my readers and I personally read every single review!I

INTRODUCTION TO THE MEDITERRANEAN DIET

Are you worried about your health and want to start a way of eating that will somewhat protect you from most life-threatening diseases? Do you want to be in shape or stay fit and avoid the health conditions brought on by obesity? You are probably aware of the health dangers of being overweight and obese. It could cause a wide range of diseases, including cardiovascular diseases, diabetes, high blood pressure, and inflammatory problems.

The concern is that according to a recent report, over half of the population worldwide will become overweight or obese in over a decade, around 2035. The 2023 atlas of the World Obesity Federation forecasts around 51 percent of the world, or over 4 billion people, are prone to becoming overweight or obese in the next 10 to 12 years—that is, if you don't do something about it or act on it.

How can you prevent that from happening to you? Is there a way for you, and maybe your loved ones, to stay healthy and maintain a fit body? The answer is yes. The only thing that you have to do is to watch out for what you put inside your body. This means that you should start changing how you eat and be disciplined and committed enough to stick to a healthy diet. And one way to make that happen is to stick to and follow the Mediterranean diet, which has gained extreme popularity because of the many good things it can do for the body.

As the name suggests, this diet plan revolves around sticking to the traditional eating habits followed by those in the Mediterranean region. I find it healthy and good for the body as it is based mainly on plants. In other words, it emphasizes the intake of fruits, vegetables, legumes, seeds, nuts, and whole grains—all of which are already known for being rich in nutrients and low in calories.

Seafood and fish are also vital components of this diet plan. It also allows you to consume dairy products, like yogurt and cheese, but in moderate amounts. The same applies to eggs and poultry, as you must eat them in moderation. As for sweets and red meat, there is no need to ban them completely from your diet plan, but you have to consume them in very limited amounts.

One thing that gives the Mediterranean diet an edge over the other diet plans is that it is not solely about what you eat. It also puts emphasis on how you eat. It provides a lot of importance to cooking, preparing food at home, and sharing and enjoying food with loved ones. Since the Mediterranean region considers red wine its traditional drink, it should also be consumed in this diet, though you have to do so moderately. If the particular way of eating encouraged in the Mediterranean diet interests you, then this e-book is perfect for you; you'll get everything that you need to learn about the Mediterranean diet. It will enlighten you as to the benefits that you can gain from this diet plan, especially when it comes to the following:

- Fighting obesity. The fact that the Mediterranean diet focuses more on eating nutrient-dense and fiber-rich foods means it can also help fight unwanted weight gain and obesity. I noticed how the foods in this diet plan are so filling and satisfying that they leave less room for binge eating and unnecessary snacking. This can further result in lower calorie intake and healthy weight loss.
- Preventing high blood pressure. The reason behind this is the high potassium content of the foods in the Mediterranean diet. This makes it effective in counteracting the negative effects of sodium on the body and reducing blood pressure.
- Improving cardiovascular health. Anyone following this diet plan can also lower their risk of cardiovascular diseases. It can improve blood lipid levels, stimulate better and healthier blood vessel function, and lower inflammation.

I have been a proponent of this diet plan for a couple of years and noticed how it helped improve my overall health. Aside from the mentioned benefits, the Mediterranean diet also contributes to improving insulin sensitivity, preventing Type 2 diabetes by regulating blood sugar levels, and fighting inflammation. After I started following this diet plan, I also noticed a big improvement in my cognitive function and mental health. It is mainly because of the anti-inflammatory properties present in this diet plan and the nutrient-dense foods designed to support the workings of the brain.

I experienced firsthand how good the Mediterranean diet is for improving one's health. It is a balanced and healthy way of eating that will help address various health problems. And you will get to know more about it as you continue reading this book.

What's so great about this Mediterranean diet book is that it gives the most important details about this diet plan and how to use it to your best advantage. You will learn more about how to make it work, especially when boosting your overall health and fighting diseases. You will learn about its principles and guidelines presented in a straightforward and easy-to-understand manner, which is a huge help if you want to have an easier time transitioning to this eating habit and lifestyle.

This book provides comprehensive information about the Mediterranean diet, providing a solid foundation about what makes it unique and why it is considered a beneficial and healthy way of eating. It also imparts practical advice and tips on incorporating this eating pattern into your life. You may also love the customizable approach of this book, which means that it will help in tailoring the Mediterranean diet, so it can also meet your specific needs and make it work for you based on your preferences and lifestyle.

In addition, you will learn about several recipes you can incorporate into your Mediterranean diet. This will give you an idea of what foods to prepare without straying away from the good eating habits that this diet plan emphasizes. All the recipes here are delicious, so you will feel motivated to continue with the Mediterranean diet and avoid feeling deprived.

After reading this Mediterranean diet book, you will be more enlightened about this diet. You will also feel more motivated and inspired to make this diet plan a part of your life as soon as possible since you will be greeted by information about its benefits and the delicious recipes you can prepare.

If you are ready to experience a fun and interesting culinary journey through the traditions and flavors of the Mediterranean, then it is definitely time to get a copy of this book. With all the information here and the delicious recipes you can easily follow, you can surely recreate the Mediterranean region's healthy and vibrant dishes in your own kitchen.

The good news is that the recipes here are so easy to follow that it does not matter whether you are a beginner or someone skilled in the kitchen. Regardless of your culinary abilities, you will surely feel inspired and excited as you browse through each page of the book. So don't wait any longer. Get a copy of this book now and start exploring the delicious world of Mediterranean cuisine while feeling good about yourself, as this journey also brings you closer to better health and physique.

Potential Health Benefits of the Mediterranean Diet

Did you know that Sardinians, along with several nations of the Mediterranean region, have the longest life expectancy in the world? According to the statistics, chronic disease rates, such as cardiovascular diseases, Type 2 diabetes, and obesity, have been low in the Mediterranean region.

There are many ways to discuss dieting and nutrition in all their complexity, but I like to keep it simple: What foods come to mind when you think of a healthy diet? The Mediterranean dietary pyramid is pretty straightforward: high consumption of whole grains, vegetables, fruits, and herbs; moderate consumption of seafood, nuts, seeds, and red wine; low consumption of poultry, eggs, cheese, and yogurt. In fact, both major points, ingredients and healthy cooking techniques, need to be considered. When we cook healthy foods in the wrong way, they will lose nutrients and become harmful to our health. Let's say you want to cook shrimp. Shrimp is low in calories and rich in protein, selenium, vitamin B12, and antioxidants, which reduce inflammation.

On the other hand, frying in deep oil drastically increases its caloric value and produces toxic chemicals that have been shown to cause inflammation and oxidative damage. It leads to metabolic acidosis linked to a greater risk of malignancy. Therefore, opt for grilled, poached, baked, or pan-seared fish, and use a few drizzles of heart-healthy olive oil for your pan. Even people who rarely cook at home can reap significant health benefits when following some basic principles of the Mediterranean diet.

Besides being good sources of fiber and vitamins, most vegetables, fruits, and legumes have a low glycemic index (GI), which means that they have an insignificant effect on blood sugar levels and glucose concentration; consequently, they can lower high insulin levels and bad cholesterol levels, as well as reduce Type 2 diabetes-related health complications. As you probably already know, high insulin levels are linked to insulin resistance and weight gain. Many studies suggest that fiber-rich diets can offer significant protection against several serious diseases. Plus, foods naturally high in fiber are typically lower in calories and have larger water content. On the other hand, water-rich foods such as veggies and fruits will keep you full longer, maintaining your healthy body mass. It is well known that obesity drastically increases the risk of stroke, osteoarthritis, sleep apnea, and premature death.

When it comes to weight loss, most of us experience weight cycling, also known as the yo-yo effect, rapidly gaining weight after a successful diet. It seems much easier to lose weight than maintain it. The secret to losing and maintaining healthy body weight lies in finding a lifelong healthy diet. You will need good-quality, nutrition-dense foods to boost metabolism and induce fat-burning while maintaining your muscle mass and keeping your well-being in balance.

Here is how you can lose weight on the Mediterranean diet:

1. Caloric deficit. First and foremost, you should create a calorie deficit. It won't be a problem on the Mediterranean diet since you are allowed to eat a lot of plant-based and low-calorie foods while avoiding saturated fats and bad carbohydrates. Obviously, bad carbs are high in calories and low in fiber and nutrition, so they are not beneficial for your health and healthy weight. Plus, they digest fast, so you get hungry quickly. Unlike bad carbs, good carbs such as fruit, vegetables, and whole grains are full of nutrients. They digest slowly and help your blood sugar remain steady.

2. Stay hydrated. A good rule of thumb is pretty straightforward: drink water when you're thirsty. We can get water from foods and beverages, such as tea, juices, fruits, and vegetables. The Mediterranean diet also encourages drinking herbal teas such as chamomile, mint, and sage. You can also consume green tea, one of the most effective beverages for weight loss; it can decrease both weight and body fat.

3. Exercise. If you look at the Mediterranean diet as a way of life, not a restrictive diet plan, you are more likely to include regular exercise in your daily routine. In addition to quality food, workout routine has been shown to drastically improve our health. Exercise can help you lose weight, maintain ideal body mass, improve mental and cognitive function, and lower the risk of chronic disease. (Keep in mind that the Mediterranean pattern of eating was accompanied by a fairly active lifestyle, spending time in nature with family and friends.)

Numerous studies have proven that eating Mediterranean can reduce the risk of serious chronic diseases such as Type 2 diabetes, arteriosclerosis, obesity, and cancer. Chronic disease rates are lower in Mediterranean nations than in other Western populations. Knowing what your food contains and planning will help you make better food choices. Trust me, healthy eating doesn't have to be monotonous and time-consuming—you will adore the diversity of Mediterranean cuisine. This dietary regimen is endlessly adaptable, so once you get the hang of it, you will create your own culinary masterpieces.

CHAPTER 1
BREAKFAST RECIPES

Easy Matcha Pancakes

PREP TIME: 5 min
COOK TIME: 20 min
TOTAL TIME: 25 min
SERVES: 4

NUTRITIONAL FACTS
Calories: 305; Fat: 13g;
Carbs: 39.9g; Protein: 8.7g;
Sugars: 11.9g; Fiber: 4.2g

INGREDIENTS

- 1 ½ cups of gluten-free baking flour
- 2 tablespoons of premium matcha powder from Japan
- 1 ½ tsp baking powder without aluminum
- 2 eggs (optional)
- 2 tablespoons of organic granulated white cane sugar or brown rice syrup
- 1 ¼ to 1 ½ mashed ripe bananas
- 1 teaspoon organic vanilla extract
- 1 cup of almond milk without sugar
- ¾ cup dark, premium chocolate chips
- coconut oil spray, nonstick

Toppings
- Kinako flour (optional)
- authentic maple syrup (optional)

DIRECTIONS

1. In a big bowl, combine the flour, matcha, and baking soda. The almond milk, brown rice syrup, banana, vanilla, and eggs (if used) should all be combined in a different medium bowl. After combining the wet and dry ingredients with a gentle whisk, mix in the chocolate chips.
2. Using nonstick cooking spray, preheat a sizable nonstick skillet over medium heat. Two to three pancakes can be made by adding 1/4 cup of batter to the skillet at a time and frying them for two minutes, or until the bottoms are golden brown.
3. About two minutes after flipping, fry the pancakes on the opposite side till it turns golden brown as well.

Green Shakshuka

PREP TIME: 10 min
COOK TIME: 20 min
TOTAL TIME: 30 min
SERVES: 4

NUTRITIONAL FACTS
Calories: 215; Fat: 15.3g;
Carbs: 12.2g; Protein: 8.1g;
Sugars: 4.3g; Fiber: 5.4g

INGREDIENTS

- 2 tablespoons of extra-virgin olive oil
- 1 minced onion
- 2 minced garlic cloves
- 1 minced jalapeño pepper (seeded)
- 1 pound of spinach (thawed if frozen)
- 1 teaspoon of dried
- 2 tablespoons of extra-virgin olive oil
- 1 minced onion
- 2 minced garlic cloves
- 1 minced jalapeño pepper (seeded)
- 1 pound of spinach (thawed if frozen)
- 1 teaspoon of dried cumin
- ¾ teaspoon of coriander
- salt and black pepper to taste
- 2 tablespoons of harissa
- ½ cup of vegetable broth
- 8 large eggs
- chopped fresh parsley, cilantro, and red-pepper flakes for serving (as desired)

DIRECTIONS

1. Set the oven's temperature to 350°F.
2. Heat the olive oil to a medium temperature in a sizable oven-safe skillet.
3. Add the onion and cook for about 4 minutes or until it is soft.

If using fresh spinach, sauté for about 4–5 minutes until fully wilted; if using frozen spinach, cook for about 1–2 minutes until cooked through Add the garlic and jalapeño, and continue to sauté for another minute until aromatic.

1. Harissa, cumin, coriander, salt, and pepper are used to season the mixture. Cook until aromatic for approximately 1 minute.
2. Place the mixture in a blender and purée until it is grainy. When the mixture is thick and smooth, add the broth and purée.

Steel-Cut Oatmeal Berry Breakfast Bake

PREP TIME: 15 min
COOK TIME: 1 h
TOTAL TIME: 1h 15 min
SERVES: 9

NUTRITIONAL FACTS
Calories: 214; Fat: 5.7g;
Carbs: 35g; Protein: 7g;
Sugars: 12.7g; Fiber: 6g

INGREDIENTS

- ½ cup dry quinoa
- ½ cup steel-cut oats
- 3 bananas (medium size)
- 1 ½ cups fresh blueberries
- 1 ½ cups fresh raspberries
- ¼ cup unsweetened coconut flakes
- 2 cups milk
- 1 scoop protein powder
- 1 ½ tablespoon maple syrup
- 1 teaspoon pure vanilla extract, no sugar added
- 1 teaspoon cinnamon, ground
- 1 pinch salt
- 2 pinches cooking spray, non-stick
- 2 large eggs

DIRECTIONS

1. Rinse and drain quinoa and oats.
2. Slice bananas and wash and drain berries, and toast coconut.
3. Prepare a liquid mixture of milk, eggs, protein powder, maple syrup, vanilla, cinnamon, and salt.
4. Preheat the oven to 375 °F. and spray a 8x8 inch square baking dish with cooking spray.
5. Arrange half of the banana slices, blueberries, and raspberries in an even layer on the bottom of the dish, then top with the rinsed quinoa and steel-cut oats.
6. Add the remaining fruit on top, then slowly pour the liquid mixture into the corner of the dish.
7. Bake for 60 minutes and sprinkle with toasted coconut flakes, if desired.
8. Allow to cool for 45–60 minutes before slicing and serving with fat-free Greek yogurt.

Sweet Potato Fritters

PREP TIME: 15 min
COOK TIME: 15 min
TOTAL TIME: 30 min
SERVES: 4

NUTRITIONAL FACTS
Calories: 414; Fat: 25.3g;
Carbs: 34.8g; Protein: 11.9g;
Sugars: 8.3g; Fiber: 5.4g

INGREDIENTS

- 1 avocado
- 1 juiced lime
- 2 teaspoons of extra virgin olive oil
- 200 g cooked, flaked, smoked, or canned salmon with fresh dill (to serve)
- 1 lime, sliced into serving-sized wedges

Fritters:
- 400 g peeled sweet potato
- sea salt and ground black pepper to taste
- 2 leaves silver beet, finely chopped
- 1 freshly chopped scallion sprig
- 2 organic eggs
- 1 teaspoon fresh coriander roughly chopped
- 2 teaspoons extra-virgin olive oil

DIRECTIONS

1. Set the oven's temperature to 150 °C/300 °F.
2. Grate the sweet potato coarsely, then put it in a basin with 1 teaspoon of sea salt to make the fritters.
3. After letting the sweet potato stand for ten minutes, drain it and squeeze out any extra juice.
4. The eggs, coriander, spring onions, and silver beet should all be placed in a separate bowl.
5. Mix thoroughly after adding the sweet potato and seasoning to taste.
6. Olive oil should be warmed in a big frying pan over medium heat.
7. Put 3 tablespoons of the mixture for each fritter into the pan and press down with a spatula as you work in 2 batches.
8. Cook for two to three minutes on each side, until golden, and then drain on paper towels.
9. While you cook the remaining fritters, place them on a baking sheet, cover them with foil, and keep them warm in the oven.
10. In a bowl, combine the lime juice and avocado flesh and mash until smooth. Add the olive oil after seasoning with salt and pepper.
11. Put two fritters on each platter before serving.
12. Add salmon, avocado, and chervil or dill sprigs on top.
13. Serve with lime wedges and drizzle with olive oil.

Chia Pudding

PREP TIME: 15 min
COOK TIME: 30 min
TOTAL TIME: 45 min
SERVES: 4

NUTRITIONAL FACTS
Calories: 305; Fat: 22.2g;
Carbs: 19.7g; Protein: 11.1g;
Sugars: 8.7g; Fiber: 8.5g

INGREDIENTS

- 375 ml almond breeze almond milk
- 4 oz soft tofu
- ½ teaspoon pure almond extract
- ¼ cup chia seeds
- ¼ cup sliced almonds
- 1 cup blueberries

DIRECTIONS

1. Blend together some almond milk, tofu, and extract in a blender until it is smooth.
2. Transfer the mixture to a bowl, and stir in some chia seeds. Let the mixture rest for 10 minutes to allow the chia seeds to absorb some of the liquid and thicken the mixture.
3. While the mixture is resting, toast some almond slices in a small skillet over low-medium heat. Stir them continuously until they are lightly golden and fragrant. Remove the skillet from the heat and set the almonds aside.
4. Gently fold in some fresh blueberries into the chia mixture. Refrigerate the pudding until it is chilled and set, about 1–2 hours.
5. When you're ready to serve, divide the chilled chia pudding evenly among four small bowls. Garnish each bowl with the toasted almonds and additional blueberries, if desired.

Masala Omelet

PREP TIME: 10 min
COOK TIME: 20 min
TOTAL TIME: 30 min
SERVES: 4

NUTRITIONAL FACTS
Calories: 195; Fat: 14.2g;
Carbs: 3.5g; Protein: 13.2g;
Sugars: 1.9g; Fiber: 0.8g

INGREDIENTS

- 8 eggs
- ½ shallot
- ¼ cup tomato fresh
- 2 cloves garlic
- ½ teaspoon salt
- 1 teaspoon turmeric
- 4 tablespoons canola oil

DIRECTIONS

1. Stir in some finely diced shallots, diced tomatoes, chopped cilantro, finely diced chilies, minced garlic, a pinch of salt, and a pinch of turmeric. Mix the ingredients well until everything is evenly combined.
2. Heat a medium-sized skillet, preferably cast iron, over high heat. Add about 1 tablespoon of oil to the pan.
3. Once the oil is hot, reduce the heat to medium and pour about a quarter of the egg mixture into the skillet. Use a spatula to evenly distribute the mixture in the pan.
4. Cover the skillet and let the omelet cook for about 2 minutes, or until the bottom is set and starting to turn golden brown.
5. Carefully flip the omelet over and cook it on the other side until it is fully set and lightly browned. Repeat the process until you have made 4 omelets in total.
6. Serve the omelets hot, garnished with additional chopped cilantro and diced tomatoes, if desired.

Mediterranean Hummus Toast with Za'atar

PREP TIME: 5 min
COOK TIME: 5 min
TOTAL TIME: 10 min
SERVES: 2

NUTRITIONAL FACTS
Calories: 427; Fat: 31.2g;
Carbs: 30.3g; Protein: 9.2g;
Sugars: 8.3g; Fiber: 6.6g

INGREDIENTS

- 2 slices of whole grain toast
- ½ cup of Sabra Roasted Pine Nut Hummus (or another flavor of your choice), divided
- 3 tablespoons of chopped greens (such as microgreens, spinach, or arugula)
- ½ cup of cherry tomatoes, diced
- ¼ of an English cucumber, diced
- 2 tablespoons of fresh parsley, chopped
- 3 green onions, chopped (both green and white parts)
- 1 tablespoon of extra virgin olive oil
- 1 tablespoon of lemon juice
- 2 teaspoons of za'atar
- 2 tablespoons of feta cheese, crumbled

DIRECTIONS

1. The diced tomato, cucumber, parsley, and green onion should all be combined in a small bowl and stirred to blend.
2. Stir the lemon juice and olive oil together in the bowl. Separate the mixture.
3. Use a toaster to toast the bread to the appropriate level.
4. Each of the two slices of bread should have an even layer of hummus on it.
5. Add the greens evenly on top of the hummus.
6. Each piece of bread should be topped with a dollop of tomato salad, some feta cheese, and za'atar.

NOTE: For added protein and flavor, try adding some sliced grilled chicken, shrimp, or tofu to the toast.
To make the toast more flavorful, try spreading a layer of pesto or tapenade on the bread before adding the hummus.
For a healthier twist, try using whole wheat or whole grain bread in place of white bread. You could also try using grain-free bread like almond or coconut flour bread.

Amaranth Oatmeal with Roasted Pears

PREP TIME: 5 min
COOK TIME: 25 min
TOTAL TIME: 30 min
SERVES: 1

NUTRITIONAL FACTS
Calories: 555; Fat: 27.3g;
Carbs: 76.2g; Protein: 15.6g;
Sugars: 33g; Fiber: 8.2g

INGREDIENTS

Oatmeal
- ½ cup uncooked amaranth
- ½ cup water
- 1 cup 2% milk
- ¼ teaspoon salt

Pears
- 1 teaspoon maple syrup
- 1 large pear
- ½ teaspoon ground cinnamon
- ¼ teaspoon ground ginger
- ⅛ teaspoon ground nutmeg
- ⅛ teaspoon ground clove

Pecan/Pear Topping
- 2 teaspoons pecan pieces
- 1 teaspoon pure maple syrup
- 1 cup plain 0% Greek yogurt, for serving

DIRECTIONS

1. Preheat the oven to 400 °F.
2. Rinse and drain the amaranth, then combine it with milk, water, and salt in a pot. Bring the mixture to a boil, then reduce the heat to low and simmer for 25 minutes until the amaranth is soft, but there is still some liquid left. Allow the amaranth to sit for 5–10 minutes to thicken, then add more milk to thin the texture if desired.
3. In a separate bowl, toss the pecan pieces with 1 teaspoon of maple syrup, then roast them in the oven until they are toasted, and the maple syrup has dried, about 10–15 minutes.
4. Dice the pears and toss them with the remaining 1 teaspoon of maple syrup and spices, then roast them in a roasting pan for 15 minutes until they are tender.
5. Stir three-quarters of the roasted pears into the oatmeal, then divide the oatmeal into two bowls and top with the roasted pecans and remaining pear pieces.

Mozzarella, Basil & Zucchini Frittata

PREP TIME: 5 min
COOK TIME: 30 min
TOTAL TIME: 35 min
SERVES: 4

NUTRITIONAL FACTS
Calories: 405; Fat: 25.5g; Carbs: 22.3g; Protein: 23.3g; Sugars: 12.2g; Fiber: 9.3g

INGREDIENTS

- 2 tablespoons Extra virgin olive oil
- 1 ½ cups red onion cut thinly
- 1 ½ cups chopped zucchini
- 7 large beaten eggs
- 2 tablespoons Extra virgin olive oil
- 1 ½ cups red onion cut thinly
- 1 ½ cups chopped zucchini
- 7 large beaten eggs
- ½ teaspoon of salt
- ¼ teaspoon of freshly ground pepper
- 2/3 cup (about 4 ounces) pearl-size or baby fresh mozzarella balls
- 3 tablespoons of soft, diced sun-dried tomatoes
- ¼ cup fresh basil, finely sliced

DIRECTIONS

1. In a sizable nonstick or cast-iron skillet that is safe for broiling, heat oil over medium-high heat. Cook the onion and zucchini for 3 to 5 minutes, stirring regularly.
2. In the meantime, whisk the salt, pepper, and eggs in a bowl. Pour the egg mixture over the ingredients in the skillet.
3. Bake your frittata in the preheated oven at 380 °F for about 20 minutes, until the edges are set.
4. Sprinkle mozzarella and sun-dried tomatoes over top and continue to bake for 3 minutes more, until cheese has melted. Add basil on top.
5. Use a spatula to lift or slide the frittata onto a chopping board or serving dish after releasing it from the pan. Serve after cutting into 4 slices.

Mediterranean Strata

PREP TIME: 10 min
COOK TIME: 55 min
TOTAL TIME: 1 h 5 min
SERVES: 4

NUTRITIONAL FACTS
Calories: 490; Fat: 23.3g; Carbs: 47.8g; Protein: 25.5g; Sugars: 13.3g; Fiber: 6.7g

INGREDIENTS

- 3 teaspoons of butter
- 2 chopped garlic cloves
- 2 minced shallots
- 1 cup of sliced button mushrooms
- 1 teaspoon of marjoram leaves, dried
- 6 cups white bread, cut into ½ inch pieces
- ½ cup of artichoke hearts, cut into 1/8 ths
- ¼ cup of Kalamata olives
- ¼ cup of marinated sun-dried tomatoes, slivered
- ¼ cup of shredded Parmesan cheese, plus additional for topping
- 4 ounces (or 1 cup) of Ciliegine Fresh Mozzarella cheese balls, halved
- 6 eggs
- 1 ½ cups of half-and-half
- ¼ cup of basil leaves, slivered
- kosher salt to taste

DIRECTIONS

1. Begin by melting 1 tablespoon of butter. Use it to lightly brush the insides of four 1-cup baking dishes (or a 2-quart baking dish, if serving family-style). Set the oven to 325 °F.
2. The remaining 2 tablespoons of butter should be melted in a sizable skillet over medium heat. Sauté the shallot and garlic for two minutes after adding them. After that, add the marjoram and mushrooms and simmer for an additional 4 minutes. After turning off the heat, pour the mushroom mixture into a sizable mixing basin.
3. Add the bread chunks, artichoke hearts, Kalamata olives, sun-dried tomatoes, Parmesan cheese, and Fresh Mozzarella to the bowl with the mushroom mixture. Stir everything together to combine, and season lightly with kosher salt. Divide the bread mixture evenly among the prepared baking dishes.
4. Combine the eggs and half-and-half in a 4-cup liquid measuring cup. Each baking dish should have 1 cup of egg mixture distributed evenly over the bread. Basil and additional Parmesan cheese are sprinkled on top of each dish.
5. The strata should be baked for 50 minutes, or until the eggs are set, on a baking sheet. After taking the dishes out of the oven, let them five minutes to cool before serving.

Salmon and Spinach Egg Muffins

PREP TIME: 10 min
COOK TIME: 25 min
TOTAL TIME: 35 min
SERVES: 6

NUTRITIONAL FACTS
Calories: 215; Fat: 13.2g;
Carbs: 1.5g; Protein: 21.1g;
Sugars: 6.5g; Fiber: 0.2g

INGREDIENTS

- 10 eggs
- 100 g salmon
- leftover roasted vegetables
- 90 g of feta, chopped Halloumi, or cream cheese
- olive oil mist
- 2 cups of freshly chopped spinach or 2 large frozen spinach cubes

DIRECTIONS

1. Preheat your oven to 450 °F.
2. In a small bowl, whisk together the eggs and set them aside.
3. In a muffin tray, layer each muffin cup with salmon, spinach, cheese of your choice, and any leftover roasted vegetables that you have on hand.
4. Pour the egg mixture over each muffin cup, dividing it evenly among the cups.
5. Bake the muffins for 25–30 minutes, or until the eggs are cooked through (you can test this by inserting a knife into the center of a muffin; if it comes out clean, the muffins are done).
6. Store the muffins in the fridge for 2–3 days as an easy breakfast or snack.

Vegan Banana Pancakes

PREP TIME: 10 min
COOK TIME: 15 min
TOTAL TIME: 25 min
SERVES: 8

NUTRITIONAL FACTS
Calories: 220; Fat: 5.6g;
Carbs: 37.4g; Protein: 5.2g;
Sugars: 6g; Fiber: 2.8g

INGREDIENTS

- 2 tablespoons Extra 1 tablespoon of ground flaxseed
- 3 tablespoons of water
- ½ cup mashed banana, about 1 large
- 2 teaspoons of extra-virgin olive oil
- 1 teaspoon of vanilla
- ¾ cup + 2 teaspoons of almond milk
- 1½ cups whole wheat pastry flour
- ½ cup oat flour
- 2 teaspoons of baking powder
- ½ teaspoon of baking soda
- 1 teaspoon of cinnamon
- ½ teaspoon of nutmeg
- ¼ teaspoon sea salt
- maple syrup, banana slices, and pecans, for serving

DIRECTIONS

1. Combine the flaxseed, water, and banana in a big bowl. Blend by mashing and stirring thoroughly 5 minutes should pass so that the mixture can thicken. Whisk in the almond milk, vanilla, and olive oil.
2. Add the cinnamon, nutmeg, salt, baking soda, and baking powder after adding the flour. The batter should still be a little lumpy after all the ingredients have been thoroughly mixed. If the dough is too thick to scoop, add another tablespoon of almond milk.
3. Preheat a nonstick skillet or griddle over medium heat. Coat the surface with a small amount of olive oil.
4. Using a 1/3-cup measuring cup, scoop the pancake batter onto the pan. Gently spread the batter into a round shape using the back of the cup.
5. Cook the pancakes until bubbles appear on the surface, about 1½ minutes. Carefully flip the pancakes and cook for an additional 1½ minutes, or until they are golden brown on both sides. If necessary, adjust the heat to ensure that the middles of the pancakes cook without burning the outsides.
6. Serve the pancakes hot, with your choice of toppings such as maple syrup, sliced bananas, and pecans. These fluffy and flavorful pancakes are sure to become a breakfast favorite!

Cauliflower "Tabbouleh"

PREP TIME: 5 min
COOK TIME: 5 min
TOTAL TIME: 10 min
SERVES: 4

NUTRITIONAL FACTS
Calories: 47; Fat: 0.5g;
Carbs: 10g; Protein: 3.4g;
Sugars: 3.5g; Fiber: 3g

INGREDIENTS

- 12 oz. uncooked cauliflower florets
- 1 cup of packed curly parsley (including stems), roughly chopped
- 1 cup of cherry tomatoes in a variety of colors, halved
- 2 Persian cucumbers, sliced
- 3 tablespoons of fresh lemon juice
- 1/2 small red onion, nicely diced
- 1/2 teaspoon of ground cumin
- 1/2 teaspoon of kosher salt
- 1/2 teaspoon of pepper

DIRECTIONS

1. Start by preparing the cauliflower rice. Grate the cauliflower using the finest setting on a box grater, or pulse it in a food processor until it is finely chopped. You should end up with about 2 1/2 cups of cauliflower rice. Transfer it to a large mixing bowl.
2. In the food processor (or using a sharp knife), finely chop the parsley. Add it to the bowl with the cauliflower rice, along with the cherry tomatoes, cucumbers, lemon juice, red onion, ground cumin, kosher salt, and pepper. Toss everything together until well combined, and adjust the seasonings to taste.
3. For extra flavor, you could try adding some minced garlic, diced bell peppers, or crumbled feta cheese to the mix. Or, try serving the cauliflower rice with a side of grilled chicken or tofu for added protein.

Fig & Ricotta Toast

PREP TIME: 5 min
TOTAL TIME: 5 min
SERVES: 1

NUTRITIONAL FACTS
Calories: 215; Fat: 7.2g;
Carbs: 30g; Protein: 8.3g;
Sugars: 15.5g; Fiber: 2.3g

INGREDIENTS

- 1 slice of crusty whole-grain bread (1/2-inch thick)
- ¼ cup part-skim ricotta cheese
- 1 fresh or 2 dried sliced figs
- 1 teaspoon sliced almonds, toasted
- 1 teaspoon of honey
- pinch of coarse sea salt, like Maldon

DIRECTIONS

1. Begin by toasting a slice of your favorite bread until it is crispy and golden brown.
2. While the bread is still warm, top it with a generous dollop of creamy ricotta cheese.
3. Slice a few ripe figs and scatter them over the cheese, along with a handful of almonds (either whole or chopped).
4. Finish the toast with a drizzle of honey and a sprinkle of sea salt. The salt will enhance the sweetness of the figs and honey, and add an extra layer of flavor to the dish.
5. Serve the toast immediately, while the bread is still warm and the cheese is soft and melty.

Cauliflower Fritters with Hummus

PREP TIME: 25 min
COOK TIME: 35
TOTAL TIME: 1 h
SERVES: 4

NUTRITIONAL FACTS
Calories: 338; Fat: 16.1g;
Carbs: 34.1g; Protein: 16g;
Sugars: 7.5g; Fiber: 8.3g

INGREDIENTS

- 2 15-ounce cans chickpeas, divided
- 2 ½ tablespoons olive oil, divided, plus more for frying
- 1 cup onions, chopped, about ½ a small onion
- 2 tablespoons garlic, minced
- 2 cups cauliflower, cut into small pieces, about ½ a large head
- ½ teaspoon salt
- black pepper
- hummus, for topping
- diced scallion, for garnish

DIRECTIONS

1. Set the oven to 400 °F.
2. Rinse a can of chickpeas and dry with paper towels. Remove loose skins that fall off and put the chickpeas in a big dish. Combine 1 tablespoon of olive oil with the chickpeas. Avoid crowding the chickpeas when spreading them out on a sizable pan. Salt and pepper the chickpeas as desired.
3. The chickpeas should be quite crispy after 20 minutes of baking, after which they should be stirred and baked for a further 5 to 10 minutes.
4. When roasted, add the chickpeas to a large food processor and process until they are crumbled and broken down, but still, retain some structure. Put the chickpeas in a small basin and save them.
5. On medium-high heat, warm the remaining 1 1/2 tablespoons of olive oil in a big pan. For about two minutes, add the onion and garlic and sauté until just starting to turn golden. Add the chopped cauliflower and heat for another 2 minutes, or until it turns brown.
6. Reduce the heat to low and put a lid on the pan. Stirring occasionally, continue cooking until the cauliflower is soft to the fork and the onions are browned and caramelized.
7. Enter the food processor with the cauliflower mixture. Add the salt and a generous teaspoon of pepper to the food processor along with the remaining can of chickpeas after draining and rinsing them. Blend until the mixture is smooth and beginning to form a ball, pausing occasionally to scrape down the sides.
8. You don't need all the roasted chickpea crumbs, but it's simpler to break them down when you have a greater number. Add 1/2 cup of the crumbs to the cauliflower mixture in the large bowl. Stir thoroughly to mix.
9. A large pan should only have a thin layer of oil covering the bottom before it is heated on medium heat. The patties should be cooked for around 2–3 minutes, then flipped and cooked one more.
10. Add hummus and diced scallion.

Notes: 1) Choose a flavored hummus, such as roasted red pepper, for the best results. If you want the hummus to be more «saucy,» you can thin it out with a mixture of equal parts water and olive oil, until it reaches your desired consistency.
2) Coat the bottom of a large pan with a thin layer of olive oil. Use a paper towel to evenly spread the oil around the pan, but avoid using too much oil or the chicken tenders will become soggy.
3) Place the chicken tenders in the pan and cook them over medium heat. Resist the urge to flip them too frequently, as this will prevent a nice crust from forming. Instead, let the tenders cook until they are golden brown on one side, and then gently flip them using a fork (a spatula may scrape off the crust).

Baba Ganoush

PREP TIME: 15 min
COOK TIME: 50 min
TOTAL TIME: 1 h 5 min
SERVES: 3

NUTRITIONAL FACTS
Calories: 210; Fat: 13g;
Carbs: 22g; Protein: 6g;
Sugars: 11g; Fiber: 11g

INGREDIENTS

- 4 pounds eggplants
- ¼ cup of lemon juice
- 2 minced garlic cloves
- 2 tablespoons and ¼ cup of tahini paste
- 1½ teaspoons salt
- freshly ground black pepper
- ½ teaspoon ground cumin
- ⅛ teaspoon smoked paprika, plus additional for serving
- 2 tablespoons Extra virgin olive oil, plus more for serving
- Italian parsley, freshly chopped, for serving
- toasted pita bread, pita chips, and/or crudités, for serving

DIRECTIONS

1. Set a rack in the middle of the oven and preheat it to 500 °F. A baking sheet should be covered with parchment paper.
2. To stop them from popping in the oven, puncture each eggplant all over with a fork, spacing the pricks about 1½ inches apart. Place the eggplant on the baking sheet that has been prepared. Roast for 45 to 60 minutes, turning the food about every 15 minutes until it is very soft and wrinkled. When the eggplant is cold enough to handle, let it cool on the baking sheet.
3. Remove stem ends, cut lengthwise, scoop out the flesh, discard skin, and press out liquid.
4. Place strained eggplant flesh in a food processor, add oil, cumin, smoked paprika, salt, pepper, lemon juice, garlic, and tahini. Pulse the mixture for 5–10 seconds, or until it has a chunky, grainy texture. Adjust the seasoning with additional lemon juice, salt, and pepper, if needed. When ready to serve, transfer the baba ganoush to a serving bowl, wrap it in plastic wrap, and refrigerate until chilled.
5. Before serving, allow the dip to sit at room temperature for 15–20 minutes. To serve, use a spoon to create a swirl in the center of the dip and drizzle olive oil over it. Sprinkle the dip with parsley and smoked paprika and serve with toasted pita bread, pita chips, and/or crudités. It's important to mince the garlic before adding it to the food processor because the mixture only gets a few pulses in the machine.

Poached Eggs On Avocado & Feta Toast

PREP TIME: 10 min
COOK TIME: 15 min
TOTAL TIME: 25 min
SERVES: 8

NUTRITIONAL FACTS
Calories: 220; Fat: 5.6g; Carbs: 37.4g; Protein: 5.2g; Sugars: 6g; Fiber: 2.8g

INGREDIENTS

- 2 tablespoons Extra 1 2 tablespoons white wine vinegar
- 2 big eggs
- 1 avocado
- 50 g feta
- 1 teaspoon of chili flakes
- 1 teaspoon lemon juice, freshly squeezed
- 2 large slices of whole-wheat bread (preferably with seeds)

DIRECTIONS

1. Fill a large saucepan of water to a boil over high heat. Add a splash of vinegar to the water, then reduce the heat to a simmer. Use a spoon to swirl the water into a whirlpool, then carefully crack both eggs into the pan. Poach the eggs for 2 1/2 minutes, or until they reach your desired level of doneness.
2. While the eggs are cooking, mash together the avocado, feta, chili flakes, and lemon juice in a small bowl. To taste, add black pepper to the mixture. Toast your bread until it is crisp and golden.
3. Spread the avocado and feta mixture onto the toast, then top each slice with a perfectly poached egg. Serve immediately and enjoy!

Spinach-Curry Crêpes with Apple, Raisins and Chickpeas

PREP TIME: 10 min
COOK TIME: 25 min
TOTAL TIME: 35 min
SERVES: 6

NUTRITIONAL FACTS
Calories: 327; Fat: 11g; Carbs: 47g; Protein: 13g; Sugars: 13g; Fiber: 6g

INGREDIENTS

- 2 eggs
- 1/3 cup finely chopped fresh cilantro
- ¼ teaspoon black pepper
- 2 ½ cups 1% milk
- 3 tablespoons all-purpose flour
- 3 tablespoons sunflower oil
- ¾ teaspoon kosher salt
- 1 can (15.5 oz) drained and washed chickpeas
- 1 small yellow onion, diced
- 1 diced Granny Smith apple
- ¼ cup golden raisins
- 2 tablespoons Madras curry powder
- 10 oz. fresh spinach
- lemon wedges, for serving

DIRECTIONS

1. Add the following ingredients: eggs, cilantro, pepper, 1 cup of milk, 1 cup of flour, 2 tablespoons of oil, and 1/4 teaspoon of salt. Mix until smooth.
2. Next, lightly coat a 10» nonstick skillet with cooking spray and heat over medium heat. Pour 1/3 cup of the crêpe batter into the pan and cook until the edges are set, about 1 minute. Flip it and cook for an additional 30 seconds. With the remaining batter, repeat the procedure. Once all the crêpes are cooked, cover them to keep them warm until you are ready to serve.
3. Heat 1 tablespoon of oil in a skillet over medium heat. When the oil is hot, add the onion and cook until it becomes soft and translucent, about 5 minutes.
4. Next, add the chickpeas, apple, raisins, and curry powder to the skillet. Stir the mixture occasionally and cook for an additional 3 minutes. To thicken the filling, stir in the remaining 2 tablespoons of flour and cook for 30 seconds. Then, add the remaining 1 1/2 cups of milk to the skillet. Cook the mixture until it reaches a thick, creamy consistency, about 2 minutes.
5. Finally, add the spinach and the remaining 1/2 teaspoon salt to the skillet. Cook for about 2 minutes, or until the spinach has wilted.
6. To serve the crêpes, divide the filling among them, fold each in half, and serve with lemon wedges. The lemon wedges add a refreshing burst of citrus flavor to each bite.

Shakshuka

PREP TIME: 5 min
COOK TIME: 20 min
TOTAL TIME: 25 min
SERVES: 2

NUTRITIONAL FACTS
Calories: 340; Fat: 20g;
Carbs: 21g; Protein: 21g;
Sugars: 17g; Fiber: 0g

INGREDIENTS

- 1 tablespoon of olive oil
- 2 red onions
- 1 red chili, deseeded and finely sliced one red chili
- 1 garlic clove, diced; a small bunch of chopped coriander leaves and stalks
- 2 cans cherry tomatoes
- ½ teaspoon caster sugar
- 4 eggs

DIRECTIONS

1. To make a spicy tomato sauce with eggs, heat some oil in a covered frying pan. Once the oil is hot, add the onions, garlic, chili, and coriander stems to the pan. Cook for about 5 minutes, or until the vegetables are tender. Then, add the sugar and tomatoes to the pan and let the mixture bubble for 8–10 minutes until it becomes thick and saucy.
2. Dip the back of a big spoon into the sauce four times. Crack an egg into each indent and put a lid on the pan. Cook the eggs for 6–8 minutes on low heat, depending on your desired level of doneness. Serve the eggs with crusty bread and garnish with coriander leaves

Zucchini Fritters with Feta and Dill

PREP TIME: 15 min
COOK TIME: 20 min
TOTAL TIME: 35 min
SERVES: 12

NUTRITIONAL FACTS
Calories: 152; Fat: 11g;
Carbs: 8g; Protein: 5g;
Sugars: 3g; Fiber: 1g

INGREDIENTS

- 1 pound of trimmed, medium-sized zucchini
- 1 teaspoon salt
- 2 big eggs
- 2 minced scallions
- 2 tablespoons fresh dill, minced
- ½ cup crumbled feta cheese
- 1 medium garlic clove, minced or pressed with a garlic press
- ¼ teaspoon black pepper
- ¼ cup (or cornstarch) all-purpose flour
- ½ teaspoon baking powder
- 3 tablespoons olive oil, plus additional amounts as needed
- serving with slices of lemon

DIRECTIONS

1. Use a box grater with large holes to shred the zucchini, or a food processor with a shredding disk. Put the zucchini in a sieve with fine mesh over a bowl. Salt the zucchini, toss it and let it stand for ten minutes. With your hands, squeeze out all the extra juice from the zucchini, then set it aside.
2. Eggs should be beaten in a big bowl. Add the feta, scallions, dill, black pepper, and dried zucchini to the mixture. Over the mixture, sprinkle the flour (or cornstarch) and baking powder, and stir until thoroughly combined.
3. In a big non-stick skillet, heat 3 tablespoons of olive oil over medium heat. Use a spoon's back to gently press the batter into 2-inch-wide fritters by dropping bits of the batter onto the pan that are the size of a 2-tablespoon. 2–3 minutes per side, pan-fry until both sides are golden brown. Transfer the fritters to a platter covered with paper towels. Repeat with the remaining batter, if necessary, adding a little more oil to the pan. Serve with lemon wedges at room temperature or warm.
4. Freezer-Friendly Instructions: You can freeze the cooked fritters for up to three months. On a cookie sheet, rewarm them in a 200 °F oven until thoroughly warmed.

Vegan Carrot Waffles

PREP TIME: 10 min
COOK TIME: 20 min
TOTAL TIME: 30 min
SERVES: 4

NUTRITIONAL FACTS
Calories: 282; Fat: 9.1g;
Carbs: 47.3g; Protein: 6.7g;
Sugars: 13.3g; Fiber: 5.9g

INGREDIENTS
- 2 cups of white wheat mixture or whole spelled flour
- 2 teaspoons of baking powder
- 2 tablespoons blended flaxseed
- 1 teaspoon cinnamon
- 250 ml of shredded carrots in a cup
- 2 cups (500 ml) of almond milk, served warm.
- ¼ cup (60 ml) liquid coconut oil
- 1 teaspoon of vanilla extract
- 2 tablespoons maple syrup
- salt
- for serving, use maple syrup or coconut cream

DIRECTIONS
1. Preheat the waffle iron. In a large mixing bowl, combine the flour, baking powder, flaxseed, cinnamon, and a pinch of salt.
2. In a separate bowl, mix together the grated carrots, almond milk, coconut oil, vanilla, and maple syrup. Gently fold the carrot mixture into the dry ingredients, stirring until the batter is just combined.
3. Scoop an appropriate batter onto your preheated waffle iron and cook until the edges are slightly crisp. The result will be a mouthwatering waffle with a hint of cinnamon and the sweetness of maple syrup.
4. Serve these waffles hot, drizzled with maple syrup and a dollop of coconut cream for an extra creamy and indulgent touch.

Greek Yogurt Tuna Salad

PREP TIME: 10 min
TOTAL TIME: 10 min
SERVES: 4

NUTRITIONAL FACTS
Calories: 130; Fat: 1.9g;
Carbs: 5.8g; Protein: 19.9g;
Sugars: 4.2g; Fiber: 0.6g

INGREDIENTS
- 2 (140 g) cans of tuna in water
- ½ cup (120 g) plain Greek yogurt (highly advised: 2% or full fat)
- 1/3 cup (45 g) diced celery, about 1 medium rib
- 1/3 cup (45 g) red onion, finely chopped (approximately 1/4 medium onion),
- 35 g or 2 1/2 teaspoons of sweet pickle relish
- 1 teaspoon Dijon mustard
- ½ teaspoon kosher salt
- ¼ teaspoon black pepper
- pinch of cayenne pepper (optional)

DIRECTIONS
1. Prepare the celery and red onion by finely chopping them.
2. Greek yogurt, sweet pickle relish, Dijon mustard, kosher salt, black pepper, and cayenne pepper all combined in a medium bowl (if using). Blend everything together by whisking. Place aside.
3. Tuna cans should be opened. Put the tuna in the strainer with the fine mesh, and place it over a basin or the sink. To extract as much moisture from the tuna as possible, very forcefully press the tuna into the mesh. When done, the tuna should be quite dry.
4. To the bowl with the Greek yogurt mixture, add the tuna along with the finely chopped celery and red onion. To thoroughly combine the ingredients, stir with a spoon.
5. If more salt or pepper is required, taste the tuna salad and add as desired. Serve right away or let the food chill in the refrigerator, covered, for several hours or overnight for the finest flavor.

CHAPTER 2
LUNCH RECIPES

Greek Shrimps with Tomatoes and Feta

PREP TIME: 15 min
COOK TIME: 15 min
TOTAL TIME: 30 min
SERVES: 2

NUTRITIONAL FACTS
Calories: 146; Fat: 4g; Carbs: 9.7g; Protein: 18.3g; Sugars: 3.8g; Fiber: 2g

INGREDIENTS

- 1 ½ pounds jumbo shrimps, 21/25, fully thawed, peeled and deveined
- kosher salt
- black pepper
- 1 ½ teaspoons of dry oregano, divided
- 1 ½ teaspoons of dry dill weed, divided
- pinch of red pepper flakes
- 6 garlic cloves, divided and minced
- Extra virgin olive oil
- 1 large finely chopped red onion
- 1 26- ounce can of diced tomatoes, drain only some of the liquid
- ½ teaspoon lemon juice
- fresh mint leaves, finely chopped
- fresh parsley leaves, finely chopped
- 2 ounces of Greek feta cheese, or more if desired
- 6 chopped, pitted Kalamata olives (optional)

DIRECTIONS

1. To prepare the dried shrimp mixture, place the shrimp in a large bowl. Mix in ½ teaspoon of minced garlic, ½ teaspoon of dry oregano, ½ teaspoon of dry dill weed, kosher salt, pepper, and a dash of red pepper flakes to taste. Drizzle in some extra virgin olive oil and toss to combine. Set aside.
2. In a large, heavy skillet (such as a cast iron skillet), heat 2 tablespoons of extra virgin olive oil over medium heat until it shimmers but does not smoke. Add the remaining minced garlic and the chopped onion. Cook, stirring frequently, until fragrant, about a few minutes. Add the tomatoes and lemon juice, and season with a pinch of salt, pepper, and the remaining oregano and dill. Increase the heat until the mixture comes to a boil, then reduce the heat to medium-low and let it simmer for 15 minutes.
3. Add the marinated shrimps and cook for 5 to 7 minutes until they turn pink. Stir occasionally to prevent the shrimp from sticking to the pan. Avoid overcooking.
4. When the shrimps are cooked, add fresh parsley and mint leaves. Top with feta cheese and Kalamata olives. If desired, add more red pepper flakes or a squeeze of lemon juice to taste.
5. Serve the flavorful sauce over orzo, your preferred grain, or crusty bread. Enjoy!

Sweet Potato-Black Bean Burgers

PREP TIME: 15 min
COOK TIME: 30 min
TOTAL TIME: 45 min
SERVES: 4

NUTRITIONAL FACTS
Calories: 454; Fat: 22.2g; Carbs: 54g; Protein: 11.5g; Sugars: 8.8g; Fiber: 8.9g

INGREDIENTS

- 2 cups of grated sweet potato
- 1/2 cup of old-fashioned rolled oats
- 1 cup of no-salt-added black beans that have been rinsed
- 1/2 cup of chopped scallions
- 1/4 cup of vegan mayonnaise
- 1 tablespoon of no-salt-added tomato paste
- 1 teaspoon of curry powder
- 1/8 teaspoon of salt
- 1/2 cup of plain unsweetened almond milk yogurt
- 2 tablespoons of chopped fresh dill
- 2 tablespoons of lemon juice
- 2 tablespoons of extra-virgin olive oil
- 4 toasted whole-wheat hamburger buns
- 1 cup of thinly sliced cucumber

DIRECTIONS

1. Wrung out the grated sweet potato with paper towels to eliminate any extra moisture before being put in a big bowl. Pound the oats to a fine powder in a food processor before being added to the sweet potato mixture. Add the beans, scallions, mayonnaise, tomato paste, curry powder, and salt to the bowl. Use your hands to mash the ingredients together. Four 1/2-inch-thick patties made from the mixture should be formed; placed them on a plate and chilled for 30 minutes.
2. In a separate bowl, combine the yogurt, dill, and lemon juice; set it aside.
3. Heat a large cast-iron pan over medium-high heat with some oil in it. Then, add the patties and fry them for about 3 minutes per side, or until they are golden brown.
4. Equally, distribute the yogurt sauce between the top and bottom hamburger buns. Replace the top bun halves after adding a burger and several cucumber slices to each bottom bun half. Immediately serve the burgers, or cover them with parchment paper and chill them until you're ready to serve.

Paella

PREP TIME: 15 min
COOK TIME: 50 min
TOTAL TIME: 1h 5 min
SERVES: 6

NUTRITIONAL FACTS
Calories: 535; Fat: 15g;
Carbs: 59g; Protein: 37g;
Sugars: 3g; Fiber: 3g

INGREDIENTS

- 2 links cured chorizo, sliced into rounds
- 2 medium chicken breasts divided into 1» pieces
- kosher salt
- 1/2 large onion chopped
- 1 chopped red bell pepper
- pinch of saffron threads
- 3 minced garlic cloves
- 1/4 cup of dry white wine
- 1 cup of Arborio rice
- 2/3 cup of canned diced tomatoes
- 2 teaspoons of smoked paprika
- 1 1/2 cups of chicken stock
- 12 mussels cleaned and debearded
- 1/4 lb. peeled and deveined shrimps
- freshly chopped parsley, for garnish
- lemon wedges, for serving

DIRECTIONS

1. Over a medium heat source, place a sizable (10 to 12 inch) skillet. Once hot, add the chorizo and cook until it is crisp. Remove the chorizo from the skillet and set it aside. If necessary, add 1 tablespoon of olive oil to the skillet. Next, add the chicken to the skillet and cook for 6–8 minutes, or until it is cooked through and no longer pink. Season with salt and then remove the chicken from the pan.
2. In the same skillet, cook the onion and bell pepper for 6 minutes, or until they are soft. You may need to add additional olive oil to the pan as necessary.
3. While the onion and bell pepper are cooking, mix the saffron with a tablespoon of warm water in a small bowl. Stir in the garlic and simmer for an additional minute or until fragrant.
4. Deglaze the skillet by adding white wine to the pan. To get rid of any browned parts, scrape the bottom of the pan with a wooden spoon. Once the wine has evaporated, add the rice, tomatoes, and paprika to the skillet. Season with salt and pepper. Stir occasionally, letting the rice toast in the pan for 2–3 minutes, or until the spices are fragrant, and the rice is just starting to brown.
5. Add the saffron and chicken broth (mixed with water) to the pan. Bring the mixture to a simmer, then stir in the cooked chicken and chorizo. Cover the pan and cook for 12–15 minutes, or until the rice has absorbed almost all the liquid.
6. Reduce the heat, then top the rice with mussels and shrimps. Cook for an additional 1–5 minutes, or until the shrimps are fully cooked, and the mussels have opened up. Serve the dish with lemon and parsley as garnishes.

Low-Fat Turkey Bolognese

PREP TIME: 10 min
COOK TIME: 45 min
TOTAL TIME: 55 min
SERVES: 4-6

NUTRITIONAL FACTS
Calories: 267; Fat: 13g;
Carbs: 15g; Protein: 23g;
Sugars: 12g; Fiber: 6g

INGREDIENTS

- 1 pint of halved cherry
- 400g minced lean turkey (choose breast instead of thigh mince if you can, as it has less fat)
- 2 teaspoons vegetable oil
- 1 big, chopped onion
- 1 large carrot
- finely sliced three celery stalk
- finely chopped, a
- 250g container of brown mushrooms
- and a pinch of sugar
- 1 tablespoon tomato purée
- 2 cans of chopped tomato with garlic and herbs, 400g each
- 400 ml of chicken stock from 1 low-sodium stock cube
- cooked wholemeal pasta

DIRECTIONS

1. Heat a nonstick frying pan over high heat and dry-fry the turkey mince until it is browned. Once cooked, transfer the turkey to a plate and set it aside.
2. Next, add oil to the pan and sauté the onion, carrot, and celery for about 10 minutes, stirring occasionally, until they are tender. If the vegetables start to stick to the pan, add a splash of water to help them cook. Afterward, add the mushrooms and continue to cook for a few minutes. Finally, whisk in the sugar and tomato purée for one more minute to prevent sticking.
3. Season the stock and add the tomatoes, turkey, and other ingredients to the pan. Simmer the mixture until it has thickened for at least 20 minutes (or longer if desired). If you have fresh basil, serve the dish with spaghetti and garnish with basil.

Chicken Gyros with Tzatziki Sauce

PREP TIME: 10 min
COOK TIME: 10 min
MARINATING TIME: 30 min
TOTAL TIME: 50 min
SERVES: 4

NUTRITIONAL FACTS
Calories: 411; Fat: 21g;
Carbs: 10g; Protein: 44g;
Sugars: 6g; Fiber: 1g

INGREDIENTS

Greek Chicken
- 1 ½ tablespoons of lemon juice
- ½ cup of plain yogurt
- 1 ¼ tablespoons of sea salt with dried oregano and Mediterranean spices
- 1 ½ pounds of chicken tenders
- 2 tablespoons of extra-virgin olive oil
- 1 cup of Tzatziki sauce
- 4 thin Greek pita bread slices
- 4 cocktail tomatoes, quartered after being cut in half;
- ¼ red onion, thinly sliced

For the Tzatziki Sauce
- 1 cucumber, cut in half, peel and seeds removed
- ¾ cup of low-fat plain Greek yogurt
- 2 minced or pressed garlic cloves
- 1 tablespoon of red wine vinegar
- 1 tablespoon finely chopped fresh dill
- fresh black pepper, freshly ground, and a pinch of kosher salt

DIRECTIONS

1. Combine lemon juice, yogurt, and sea salt in a bowl and toss the tenders to coat evenly. Cover and refrigerate for at least 30 minutes, or overnight.
2. Heat a large non-stick skillet over medium-high heat and add 1 tablespoon of olive oil. Place half of the chicken tenders in the skillet, making sure to shake off any excess yogurt mixture. Cook for about 5 minutes, undisturbed, until browned, then flip and cook for an additional few minutes until fully cooked. Transfer the cooked tenders to a platter, add the remaining tablespoon of olive oil to the skillet, and cook the remaining tenders.
3. To make the tzatziki sauce, grate a cucumber and squeeze out the excess water using a paper towel. In a medium-sized bowl, mix the cucumber with yogurt, garlic, red wine vinegar, fresh dill, kosher salt, and black pepper. Cover and refrigerate for at least 30 minutes, or up to 3 days.
4. Warm the pita bread in a toaster oven or microwave for 30 seconds. Spread some of the tzatziki sauce onto the warm pita bread, along with sliced tomatoes, red onion, and 2 or 3 slices of chicken tenders. Fold the pita bread and wrap in parchment paper, or serve immediately.

Notes:
Another option for cooking the chicken tenders is to grill or bake them. To grill, preheat the grill to medium-high heat and cook the tenders for about 8–10 minutes, or until cooked through. To bake, preheat the oven to 375 °F and bake the tenders for about 20 minutes, or until cooked through.

Coconut Shrimp Curry

PREP TIME: 10 min
COOK TIME: 15 min
TOTAL TIME: 25 min
SERVES: 4

NUTRITIONAL FACTS
Calories: 258; Fat: 24g;
Carbs: 12g; Protein: 3g;
Sugars: 4g; Fiber: 2g

INGREDIENTS

For Shrimp Marinade
- 1 pound extra-large shrimps, deveined and skinned
- 1/4 teaspoon salt
- ¼ teaspoon freshly ground black pepper
- ¼ teaspoon cayenne pepper
- 2 tablespoons lemon juice

For the sauce
- 1 tablespoon of coconut oil
- 1 medium onion chopped
- 3 cloves of minced garlic
- 1 tablespoon of minced fresh ginger
- ½ teaspoon of freshly ground black pepper
- ½ teaspoon of salt, or to taste
- ½ teaspoon of turmeric
- 2 teaspoons of ground coriander
- 1 teaspoon of curry powder
- 14 ½ ounces of diced tomatoes
- 13 ½ ounces of coconut milk
- 2 tablespoons of cilantro (or parsley)
- cooked rice for serving

DIRECTIONS

1. To prepare the shrimps, mix them with the marinade ingredients in a small bowl. Cover the bowl with plastic wrap and place it in the refrigerator for 10 minutes to allow it to marinate.
2. While the shrimps are marinating, heat some oil in a medium-sized skillet. When the oil is hot, add the onion to the skillet and sauté it for two to three minutes, or until it becomes soft and translucent. Add the curry powder, garlic, ginger, pepper, salt, coriander, and turmeric to the skillet and cook for an additional minute.
3. Add coconut milk and diced tomatoes with all of their juices to a pot. Stir the mixture and bring it to a boil. Allow the mixture to cook for about 5 minutes, stirring occasionally. Next, add the shrimps and any marinade fluids that have accumulated to the pot. Cook for an additional 2 minutes, or until the shrimps turn pink and are fully cooked.
4. Once the dish is finished, garnish it with chopped parsley or cilantro and serve it hot with rice.

Notes: It is recommended to store the curry in the refrigerator for up to 3 days in an airtight container. For longer storage, it is suggested to freeze the curry in a shallow container, making sure it is fully chilled before sealing. The curry can be stored for up to three months as a result. When reheating the frozen curry, be sure to stir it often to ensure even thawing.

Basil Chicken with Kumquats

PREP TIME: 10 min
COOK TIME: 1 h
TOTAL TIME: 1 h 10 min
SERVES: 4

NUTRITIONAL FACTS
Calories: 297; Fat: 17.9g;
Carbs: 9.3g; Protein: 24.2g;
Sugars: 5g; Fiber: 2.9g

INGREDIENTS

- 4 chicken thighs
- 2 tablespoons of Bertolli Organic Extra Virgin Olive Oil
- 1 cup of chopped kumquats
- 1 single red onion, cut into wedges
- 1 teaspoon dried basil
- salt and pepper
- fresh basil, for garnish

DIRECTIONS

1. Preheat your oven to 400 °F. It will help ensure that the chicken cooks evenly and at the right temperature.
2. In a cast iron or oven-safe dish, place the chicken thighs, sliced kumquats, and red onion. Drizzle everything with olive oil and use your fingers to ensure everything is coated, including both sides of the chicken. It will help the chicken and vegetables to cook evenly and become tender and flavorful. Arrange the kumquats and red onion around the chicken.
3. Sprinkle the chicken with the dried basil, salt, and pepper. These seasonings will add flavor to the dish and help the chicken gets brown as it cooks.
4. Bake the chicken for 40–50 minutes. To check if the chicken is cooked through, you can use a meat thermometer to ensure that it has reached an internal temperature of 165 °F. Alternatively, you can cut into the thickest part of the chicken and ensure that the juices run clear, and the meat is no longer pink.
5. If you want the top of the chicken to be more golden, turn on the broiler for the last 5 minutes of cooking. It will give the chicken a crispy, golden finish. Just ensure to keep a close eye on the chicken while it's under the broiler, so it doesn't burn.

Notes: 1. Cast iron pans are great for cooking, as it's my favorite. The Lodge Cast Iron Pan is a recommended option, but any oven-safe pan will work.
2. You can adjust the amount of salt and pepper to suit your taste. Just be sure not to overdo it, as too much salt can overwhelm the other flavors in the dish.
3. Adding honey or maple syrup to the olive oil before coating the chicken can add a sweet and caramelized note.
4. You can add other vegetables to the dish, such as bell peppers, carrots, or potatoes. Cut them into similar-sized pieces so that they cook evenly with the chicken.

Mediterranean Stuffed Peppers

PREP TIME: 15 min
COOK TIME: 25 min
TOTAL TIME: 35 min
SERVES: 2

NUTRITIONAL FACTS
Calories: 321; Fat: 15g;
Carbs: 37g; Protein: 11g;
Sugars: 13g; Fiber: 4g

INGREDIENTS

- 1 large red pepper and 1 large yellow pepper, both halved and deseeded with the stalks left on
- 85 g of couscous
- 25 g of toasted pine nuts
- a handful of roughly chopped black olives
- 50 g of crumbled feta cheese
- 50 g of semi-dried tomato snipped (or a handful of quartered cherry tomatoes)
- 2 tablespoons of shredded basil

DIRECTIONS

1. Heat the oven to 400 °F. Place the peppers on a plate and microwave them on medium for 5 minutes, or until they are almost soft. Transfer the peppers to a baking tray, cut-side up.
2. In a separate bowl, place the couscous and cover it with 125ml of boiling water. Stir the couscous, then cover the bowl and set it aside for 10 minutes. After 10 minutes, use a fork to fluff the couscous and break it up. Mix in the pine nuts, olives, feta, tomatoes, and basil. Pile the couscous mixture into the pepper halves and bake for an additional 10 minutes.

Quick Seafood Linguine

PREP TIME: 10 min
COOK TIME: 7 min
TOTAL TIME: 17 min
SERVES: 4

NUTRITIONAL FACTS
Calories: 321; Fat: 15g;
Carbs: 37g; Protein: 11g;
Sugars: 13g; Fiber: 4g

INGREDIENTS

- 1 tablespoon of olive oil
- 1 sliced onion
- 1 sliced garlic clove
- 1 teaspoon paprika
- 400 g of canned diced tomatoes
- 1 liter of chicken stock (from a cube is fine)
- 300 g of spaghetti or linguine, roughly broken
- 240 g of frozen seafood mixture
- chopped parsley leaves, and lemon wedges for serving

DIRECTIONS

1. Heat the oil in a wok or sizable frying pan. Next, sauté the onion and garlic for five minutes, or until they are tender. Bring to a boil after adding the stock, tomatoes, and paprika.
2. Lower the temperature to a simmer, add the pasta, and cook for 7 minutes, stirring to prevent sticking. When the pasta is cooked and the seafood is well warm, stir in the seafood and season to taste. Lemon wedges should be served alongside the garnish of parsley.

Sesame-Seared Tuna

PREP TIME: 10 min
COOK TIME: 1 min
TOTAL TIME: 11 min
SERVES: 4

NUTRITIONAL FACTS
Calories: 422; Fat: 21g;
Carbs: 13g; Protein: 44g;
Sugars: 12g; Fiber: 8g

INGREDIENTS

- ¼ cup of soy sauce
- 2 teaspoons of sesame oil
- 1 teaspoon of mirin (Japanese sweet wine)
- 1 teaspoon of honey
- 1 teaspoon of rice wine vinegar
- ½ cup of sesame seeds
- 4 (6 ounce) tuna steaks
- 1 teaspoon of olive oil
- wasabi paste

DIRECTIONS

1. In a small bowl, combine the soy sauce, sesame oil, mirin, and honey. As a dipping sauce, pour half into a separate, little bowl, combine with rice wine vinegar, and set aside.
2. On a plate, spread out the sesame seeds. Apply the remaining soy sauce mixture to the tuna steaks, then press into the sesame seeds to coat.
3. Cast iron skillet filled with hot olive oil that has been heated on high heat. Steaks should be seared for about 30 seconds on each side in the pan. Serve with wasabi paste and dipping sauce.

Mackerel with Date Butter

PREP TIME: 15 min
COOK TIME: 15 min
TOTAL TIME: 30 min
SERVES: 2

NUTRITIONAL FACTS
Calories: 590; Fat: 42g;
Carbs: 19g; Protein: 32g;
Sugars: 18g; Fiber: 6g

INGREDIENTS

- 4 teaspoons (1/2 stick) of unsalted butter
- 2 teaspoons plus 2 teaspoons date syrup
- 2 mackerels cleaned and gutted at around 1 pound each
- freshly ground black pepper and kosher salt
- 1 pint of halved tiny cherry tomatoes
- 1 cup of fresh cilantro, chopped, plus extra sprigs for garnish
- 4 pitted and chopped dates
- ½ tablespoon extra virgin olive oil
- 1 lemon zest and juice, plus 1 lemon cut into thin rounds for garnish
- 1/2 teaspoon of ground cumin
- 1/2 teaspoon of paprika
- pinch of red pepper flakes

DIRECTIONS

1. Preheat your oven to 400 °F. In a small bowl, mix 2 tablespoons of date syrup with butter. Coat the exterior of each fish well with the butter mixture. Sprinkle both the inside and outside of each fish with salt and pepper.
2. Heat a large grill pan over medium-high heat. Cook the fish for 2 to 3 minutes on each side, flipping once, until it is lightly browned. Transfer the fish to a baking sheet lined with parchment paper and roast for 12 to 15 minutes, or until it is fully cooked.
3. To make the tomato-cilantro topping, combine the following ingredients in a medium bowl: tomatoes, chopped cilantro, dates, oil, cumin, paprika, red pepper flakes, and 2 tablespoons of date syrup. Season the mixture with salt and pepper to taste, and mix everything together thoroughly.
4. Serve the fish on a large plate, topped with the tomato-cilantro mixture. Garnish with lemon rounds and cilantro sprigs if desired.

Zucchini Pasta with Lemon Garlic Shrimps

PREP TIME: 10 min
COOK TIME: 5 min
TOTAL TIME: 15 min
SERVES: 4

NUTRITIONAL FACTS
Calories: 307; Fat: 14.5g; Carbs: 12.3g; Protein: 27.4g; Sugars: 8g; Fiber: 3.4g

INGREDIENTS

- 4 small zucchinis
- 30 uncooked, peeled, and deveined shrimps (1.5 pounds)
- 2 tablespoons of olive oil
- 4 garlic cloves, chopped finely
- 2 tablespoons of ghee or butter
- lemon juice and zest
- ¼ cup chicken broth or white wine
- ¼ cup parsley (minced)
- a pinch of red pepper flakes
- salt and pepper

DIRECTIONS

1. Trim the zucchini's ends after washing them. Spiralize the zucchini to create pasta. Then, put aside.
2. In a big pan, heat the oil to a medium-high temperature. Sprinkle salt and pepper over the shrimps, then arrange them in a single layer. Without stirring, cook for one minute, allowing the bottom side to get somewhat crispy.
3. Stir the shrimps for a further minute or two to cook the other side after adding the minced garlic. The shrimps can be transferred to a plate using tongs or a sizable spoon.
4. Add the white wine, red pepper flakes, lemon juice, and zest to the pan. Stirring for the first two to three minutes of simmering.
5. The pasta with zucchini should be heated through after adding the parsley and stirring for 30 seconds. Add the shrimps to the pan and stir for an additional minute. Serve right away.

Mediterranean Turkey-Stuffed Peppers

PREP TIME: 20 min
COOK TIME: 30 min
TOTAL TIME: 50 min
SERVES: 2

NUTRITIONAL FACTS
Calories: 403; Fat: 19g; Carbs: 15g; Protein: 40g; Sugars: 14g; Fiber: 5g

INGREDIENTS

- 2 red peppers
- 1 ½ tablespoons of olive oil, plus an extra drop
- 240 g of low-fat minced turkey breast
- ½ small onion, chopped
- 1 grated garlic clove
- 1 teaspoon ground cumin
- 3–4 mushrooms, sliced
- 400 g of chopped tomatoes
- 1 tablespoon of tomato purée
- 1 cube of chicken stock
- a few leaves of fresh oregano
- 60 g mozzarella, grated
- 150 g green vegetables (spinach, kale, broccoli, mangetout or green beans), to serve

DIRECTIONS

1. Set oven temperature to 370 °F. Remove the seeds, core, and stalks from the peppers after cutting them in half lengthwise. Olive oil should be drizzled over the peppers after seasoning them properly. Roast for 15 minutes after placing on a baking sheet.
2. In the interim, warm 1 tablespoon of olive oil in a large pan over medium heat. Stirring to break up the lumps as it cooks, pour the mince onto a platter.
3. After cleaning the pan, heat the remaining oil to a medium-high temperature. After cooking the onion, garlic, and mushrooms for an additional 2–3 minutes, add the cumin.
4. Return the mince to the pan and stir in the tomato purée and chopped tomatoes. Add the stock cube crumbles and simmer for three to four minutes before seasoning with oregano. After removing the peppers from the oven, stuff them as full as you can with the mince. (Don't worry if some slips out; the crispiness will be delicious.) Add the cheese on top, then re-bake for 10 to 15 minutes, or until the cheese begins to turn brown.
5. Gently place the peppers on a platter and serve them with a large serving of your favorite blanched, boiled, or steamed greens.

Baked Tilapia with Lemon

PREP TIME: 10 min
COOK TIME: 20 min
TOTAL TIME: 30 min
SERVES: 4

NUTRITIONAL FACTS
Calories: 320; Fat: 16.2g;
Carbs: 6.3g; Protein: 40g;
Sugars: 3.7g; Fiber: 1.2g

INGREDIENTS

- 1 pint of halved cherry tomatoes
- 1 big, finely sliced shallot
- 3 minced garlic cloves
- 1 small lemon, cut into rings
- 2 tablespoons of olive oil, divided
- ¾ teaspoon of kosher salt
- 4-ounce block of feta cheese
- 1 1/2 pounds of tilapia
- 1 teaspoon of Italian seasoning
- 1 pinch of red pepper flakes (optional)
- ½ teaspoon of smoked paprika
- 2 teaspoons of drained capers
- finely chopped fresh parsley or basil, for garnish
- fresh ground black pepper

DIRECTIONS

1. Preheat the oven to 425 °F.
2. Finely chop the tomatoes, shallot, and garlic. Slice the lemon into thin rounds.
3. In a 9 x 13-inch baking dish, mix together the chopped vegetables, lemon slices, 1 tablespoon olive oil, ¼ teaspoon salt, and a few grinds of black pepper. Gently fold in the feta cheese, breaking it up into large chunks as you add it to the pan.
4. With a paper towel, dry the tilapia fillets. Rub each fillet with 1 tablespoon olive oil and 1/2 teaspoon kosher salt. Place the fillets on top of the vegetables and feta in the baking dish. Sprinkle the red pepper flakes, smoked paprika, Italian seasoning, and black pepper over the top of the fillets. Scatter capers on top of the fish.
5. Bake the pan in the oven for 20–25 minutes, or until the internal temperature of the fish, as measured with a food thermometer, reaches 140 °F.
6. When serving, remove the lemon slices (or leave them in if desired) and garnish with chopped parsley.

Briam (Greek Baked Zucchini and Potatoes)

PREP TIME: 30 min
COOK TIME: 1 h 30 min
TOTAL TIME: 2 h
SERVES: 4

NUTRITIONAL FACTS
Calories: 534; Fat: 28g;
Carbs: 66g; Protein: 11g;
Sugars: 9g; Fiber: 7g

INGREDIENTS

- 2 pounds of potatoes, carefully cut and peeled
- 6 ripe tomatoes, puréed
- 4 large zucchinis, thinly sliced
- 4 small red onions, thinly sliced
- ½ cup olive oil
- 2 teaspoons freshly chopped parsley (optional)
- salt and freshly ground black pepper

DIRECTIONS

1. Preheat the oven to 400 °F (200 degrees C). Place the potatoes, zucchinis, and red onions in a large baking dish (9x13 inches or larger, or use two baking dishes if necessary).
2. Drizzle the vegetables with olive oil and sprinkle them with parsley, salt, and pepper. Pour the puréed tomatoes over the top and toss everything together until the vegetables are coated evenly.
3. Bake the vegetables for one hour, then stir them and continue cooking for an additional 30 minutes, or until they are soft, and the moisture has evaporated.
4. Serve the vegetables warm, or remove them from the oven and let them cool slightly before serving.

Vegan Spanakopita

PREP TIME: 30 min
COOK TIME: 1 h 10 min
TOTAL TIME: 1h 40 min
SERVES: 24

NUTRITIONAL FACTS
Calories: 107; Fat: 4g; Carbs: 13g; Protein: 3g; Sugars: 0g; Fiber: 0g

INGREDIENTS

- 12 ounces of chopped fresh spinach (can also use a mixture of spinach and chard)
- 1 handful of chopped scallions (about 6-7 scallion bulb pieces)
- ¼ cup of dill
- ¼ cup of parsley
- ¼ teaspoon of sea salt
- ¼ teaspoon of ground black pepper
- Olive oil or veggie broth for sautéing
- 1 pound phyllo sheets
- 1/6 -1/3 cup of olive oil for brushing the phyllo
- 1 cup of vegan feta cheese

DIRECTIONS

Turn the oven's temperature up to 350 °F.
1. In a pan, cook the scallions in broth or olive oil for 2 minutes, or until tender. After that, include the spinach and add the salt and pepper. Cook for an additional 5 minutes, or until the spinach has wilted. Turn off the heat
2. Stir the parsley and dill into the mixture. Place all the ingredients in a large bowl.
3. In a food processor, combine the drained and rinsed cashews, vinegar, water, and salt. Process until the mixture is thick and coarsely chopped.
4. Pour the cashew «feta» mixture into the bowl with the spinach and mix thoroughly
5. Pour the olive oil into a glass bowl.
6. To fit the phyllo dough to the length of your pan, measure the dough while it is still wrapped in its packet and then cut it to size. You can cut it while it is rolled up to make it easier to handle. If you have any extra dough, you can save it for later use
7. Use a pastry brush to lightly coat the bottom of a 9x13 inch baking pan with oil.
8. Next, take a sheet of phyllo dough and place it in the pan so that half of the sheet is inside the pan and the other half is hanging over the edge. Lightly brush the half of the sheet that is inside the pan with oil. Fold the top half of the sheet over the pan and repeat the process with the top half. This must be done in this manner because the phyllo sheets are larger than the pan.
9. Repeat this process, brushing each sheet with oil, for half of the phyllo sheets
10. Once you have used half of the phyllo sheets, spread the spinach mixture on top.
11. Cover the spinach mixture with the remaining phyllo sheets, brushing each one with a second coat of olive oil. Cut the dish into squares.
12. Bake for 60–70 minutes, or until the top is golden. Depending on your oven, you may need to start checking on the dish at 50 minutes.
13. Allow the dish to cool fully before slicing and serving.
Notes: 1. You can also use frozen spinach. Just make sure to press out as much water as possible from the spinach once it defrosts to avoid making the dish watery.
2. Any type of phyllo (filo) sheet will work for this recipe, but I find the thicker ones to be more convenient and easier to work with. If you can find a package labeled «thick» or «#9 thick,» those would be good options to use
Tips to prep ahead: Make the filling the previous day.

Vegetarian Moussaka

PREP TIME: 15 min
COOK TIME: 1 h 30 min
TOTAL TIME: 1 h 45 min
SERVES: 6

NUTRITIONAL FACTS
Calories: 240; Fat: 12g;
Carbs: 26g; Protein: 10g;
Sugars: 14g; Fiber: 9g

INGREDIENTS

- 2 medium eggplants
- halal salt
- 1 medium yellow onion , divided and chopped
- 8 ounces of sliced baby bellas
- 3 minced cloves of garlic
- 4 tablespoons of extra-virgin olive oil
- 1 cup of green lentils
- 14.5-ounce can of diced tomatoes
- 1 teaspoon of dried oregano
- 2 cups of water
- freshly ground black pepper
- 2 tablespoons each of butter and all-purpose flour
- 2 cups of milk
- ¾ cup of freshly grated Parmesan
- 2 large egg yolks

DIRECTIONS

1. Preheat the oven to 400 °F. Cover baking pans with paper towels and spread the eggplant rounds in a single layer on the pans. Sprinkle salt on both sides of the eggplant rounds and let them sit for 10 minutes. Then, use paper towels to pat the eggplants dry.
2. Place the eggplant rounds in a single layer on the baking pans and brush them with 2 tablespoons of oil. Bake for 12 minutes or until the eggplants are tender.
3. Heat the remaining 2 tablespoons of oil in a large pot over medium heat. Cook the mushrooms and onion for 5 minutes, or until they are fork-tender. Add the garlic and cook for an additional minute, or until it is fragrant. Add the lentils, tomatoes, and water to the pot and season with oregano, salt, and pepper. Simmer the lentils for 30 minutes, or until they are soft. If the sauce becomes too thick, add more water as needed.
4. In a separate medium pot, melt the butter over medium heat. Add the flour and cook for one minute. Gradually pour in the milk while whisking to remove any lumps. Cook the mixture for about 5 minutes, or until it thickens. Stir in the Parmesan cheese until it is melted and well combined.
5. In a small dish, gently whisk the egg yolks. Add about 2 tablespoons of the béchamel sauce to the yolks and whisk to combine. Pour the mixture back into the béchamel and whisk to blend.
Season with pepper and salt to your desired level of flavor. Allow the sauce to simmer for 5 minutes, or until it has thickened.
6. Arrange the eggplant rounds in a single layer in a 9» x 13» baking dish. Add half of the lentil mixture to the eggplants, and repeat the layers with more eggplants and the remaining lentils. Top the dish with a final layer of eggplants. Cover the eggplants with the béchamel sauce and sprinkle the remaining 1/4 cup of Parmesan.
7. Bake the dish for 30 minutes, or until the top is brown and well heated

Creamy Tomato Risotto

PREP TIME: 5 min
COOK TIME: 35 min
TOTAL TIME: 40 min
SERVES: 4

NUTRITIONAL FACTS
Calories: 381; Fat: 10g;
Carbs: 61g; Protein: 13g;
Sugars: 9g; Fiber: 4g

INGREDIENTS

- 400 g can of chopped tomatoes
- 4 cups (1 liter) of vegetable stock
- 1 knob of butter
- 1 tablespoon of olive oil
- 1 finely chopped onion
- 2 finely chopped garlic cloves
- 1 sprig of finely chopped rosemary
- 250 g of risotto rice
- 300 g of cherry tomatoes, halved
- a small pack of roughly torn basil
- 4 tablespoons of grated Parmesan

DIRECTIONS

1. Combine the chopped tomatoes with half of the stock and process in a food processor until smooth. Combine the mixture with the remaining stock in a saucepan, then boil gently over low heat.
2. Melt the butter and oil in a big saucepan over low heat in the next step. After adding it, sauté the onion for 6 to 8 minutes, or until tender. After adding the rosemary and garlic, simmer for another minute. For one minute, stir-fry the rice after adding it.
3. Gradually add the hot stock and tomato mixture to the rice mixture while stirring frequently. Add the cherry tomatoes after adding half of the stock. Cook for 20 to 25 minutes, or until the cherry tomatoes are softened, the rice is creamy and tender, and the stock has been completely absorbed.
4. Cover the pan, wait one minute, and then add the basil. Serve the risotto with a generous amount of freshly ground black pepper and Parmesan cheese.

Roasted Garlic Vegan Cheese Fritters

PREP TIME: 5 min
COOK TIME: 15 min
TOTAL TIME: 20 min
SERVES: 12

NUTRITIONAL FACTS
Calories: 115; Fat: 5.7g;
Carbs: 14g; Protein: 2.5g;
Sugars: 2.7g; Fiber: 0.9g

INGREDIENTS

- 12 cloves of garlic
- 1 little leek
- 15-ounce can of chickpeas
- 7 tablespoons of dietary yeast
- 4 tablespoons of vegan Parmesan
- salt and pepper to taste

DIRECTIONS

1. Start by peeling and mincing the garlic cloves and washing and chopping the leek into small pieces. Heat a small amount of oil in a pan, or use vegetable broth if you prefer an oil-free dish, and fry the garlic and leek until they start to turn brown.
2. Next, place the chickpeas, nutritional yeast, garlic, vegan Parmesan, salt, and pepper in the bowl of a food processor or blender. Blend the ingredients together until they are well combined, but not completely smooth.
3. Finally, mix the leek and chickpeas together in a bowl and use your hands to form small fritters. Place the fritters on a baking sheet and bake them for about 15 minutes at 400 °F, or you can fry them in a pan over medium heat until they are golden brown.

Tofu Stir-Fry with Peanut Sauce

PREP TIME: 15 min
COOK TIME: 20 min
TOTAL TIME: 35 min
SERVES: 4

NUTRITIONAL FACTS
Calories: 504; Fat: 35g;
Carbs: 19g; Protein: 21g;
Sugars: 4g; Fiber: 7g

INGREDIENTS

- 1 tablespoon grated or chopped fresh ginger
- 1 big clove of minced garlic
- ½ of organic peanut butter (unsalted)
- ¼ cup of low-sodium soy sauce
- ¼ cup of water
- 2 tablespoons of Chinese black vinegar, (or 3 tablespoons apple cider vinegar)
- 1 teaspoon of sambal oelek or sriracha, plus additional sauce to taste
- 2 tablespoons of toasted sesame oil
- 2 tablespoons of Canola oil
- 1 (14 oz) cut into 1-inch cubes, drained, and packaged extremely firm tofu
- 2 cups of rough-cut cabbage
- 1 little head of broccoli (cut into florets)
- peanut sauce in one batch
- thinly sliced green onions, optional sesame seed

DIRECTIONS

1. Blend all the ingredients together in a food processor or blender for about 30 seconds until the mixture is smooth, cohesive, and creamy. The sauce can be made a few days in advance and stored in the refrigerator until it is ready to be used.
2. Heat a large skillet or wok over medium-high heat and add some oil. Once the oil is warm, add the tofu to the skillet and fry it for a few minutes on each side for a total of 10 to 12 minutes, or until it becomes crispy. Remove the tofu from the skillet and place it on a plate lined with paper towels to absorb any excess oil.
3. After the tofu has been cooked and removed from the skillet, add the cabbage and broccoli to the same skillet and cook for about 8 minutes, or until the vegetables are soft and tender. Once the vegetables are cooked, return the tofu to the skillet and reduce the heat to medium-low. Pour the peanut sauce over the tofu and vegetables and stir everything together until the tofu and vegetables are coated in the sauce. Allow the mixture to simmer for an additional 1–2 minutes.
4. Serve the tofu and vegetables plain, or with a side of steamed brown rice or noodles.

Notes:
   This peanut sauce has a salty flavor, which may be different from the sweet peanut sauces you are used to. While the sauce may appear very salty on its own, it will become balanced and enjoyable when it is mixed with tofu and unseasoned vegetables. If you would like the sauce to be a little bit sweeter, you can add 1 teaspoon of honey to it.

Mediterranean Chicken Quinoa Bowl with Broccoli and Tomato

PREP TIME: 10 min
COOK TIME: 30 min
TOTAL TIME: 40 min
SERVES: 3

NUTRITIONAL FACTS
Calories: 481; Fat: 23g;
Carbs: 45g; Protein: 24g;
Sugars: 2g; Fiber: 7g

INGREDIENTS

For the Chicken
- 6 ounces of skinless, boneless chicken breast
- 1/4 cup plus 2 teaspoons olive oil
- 1 lemon, squeezed and zest removed
- 2 minced or pressed garlic cloves
- 1/2 teaspoon kosher salt
- 1/4 teaspoon freshly ground black pepper
- 2 tablespoons dried oregano
- 1/2 cup of easy-to-roast tomatoes
- 1 cup of easy-to-roast broccoli and feta

For the Quinoa
- 1 teaspoon of kosher salt
- 1 cup of dried quinoa
- crumbled feta cheese

DIRECTIONS

1. To prepare the chicken, cut it into 1-inch pieces and place it in a gallon freezer bag. Combine olive oil, lemon juice and zest, garlic, oregano, salt, and pepper in a small bowl. Pour the mixture over the chicken in the bag, seal it, and marinate the chicken for at least 30 minutes or up to overnight.
2. To cook the chicken, heat 2 tablespoons of olive oil in a non-stick skillet over medium-high heat. Add the marinated chicken to the skillet and cook it for 10 to 12 minutes, or until it is fully cooked and browned on both sides.
3. To cook the broccoli and tomatoes, you may add more oil to the pan and lower the heat to medium.
4. In the meantime, prepare the quinoa by rinsing it under cold water in a fine mesh strainer. Bring a saucepan of water to a boil over high heat, then add 1 teaspoon of kosher salt and the quinoa. Boil the quinoa for 8 to 10 minutes, stirring regularly, until it is al dente. Once it is cooked, drain the quinoa, fluff it with a fork, and return it to the pot. Cover the pot with a lid and let the quinoa sit for 5 to 10 minutes.
5. To assemble the bowls, divide the quinoa evenly among them and top each bowl with half of the chicken and vegetable mixture. For flavor, add extra kosher salt, freshly ground black pepper, and olive oil to taste. Before serving, sprinkle feta cheese crumbles on top of each bowl.

Notes: The roasted broccoli and tomatoes can be prepared in advance and stored in the refrigerator for up to 3 days. To serve, add them to the cooked chicken and rewarm the mixture just before assembling the quinoa bowls.

CHAPTER 3
DINNER RECIPES

Eggplant Parmigiana Lasagna

PREP TIME: 20 min
COOK TIME: 1h
TOTAL TIME: 1 h 20 min
SERVES: 6

NUTRITIONAL FACTS
Calories: 352; Fat: 22g; Carbs: 27g; Protein: 17g; Sugars: 14g; Fiber: 10g

INGREDIENTS

- 3 (about 350g each) eggplants, cut into 1 cm-thick slices
- 1 tablespoon of olive oil
- 1 small brown onion, diced finely
- 2 garlic cloves, smashed
- 700 g bottle of passata
- 500 g tub of smooth ricotta
- 70 g (1 cup) of finely grated Parmesan
- 6 fresh lasagna sheets
- 50 g (½ cup) finely shredded mozzarella
- fresh oregano, to serve

DIRECTIONS

1. The oven should be preheated to 380 °F, fan forced. A large frying pan should be heated to medium-high. Slices of eggplant should be sprayed with oil. Cook the eggplant in batches for 3–4 minutes on each side, or until tender and golden. Place on a plate.
2. Heat oil in a pan at medium heat. Put the onion in. Cook the mixture for 4 minutes, stirring occasionally. Cook garlic while stirring for 1 minute, or until fragrant. Then, add the passata and 1/3 cup of water to the pan, swirling and pouring the mixture from the passata bottle. Mix everything together and bring it to a boil. Lower the heat and let it simmer for 5 minutes, or until it thickens slightly. Lastly, adjust the seasoning to your liking
3. Mix the Parmesan and ricotta together in a bowl. Pour 1/3 of the tomato mixture evenly over the bottom of a 23 cm ovenproof dish with a depth of 5 cm. 2 pasta sheets, trimmed to fit, are layered over the sauce. On top of the pasta, arrange a third of the eggplant. Place half of the ricotta mixture on top. Make the surface slick. Repeat with 2 additional spaghetti sheets, the remaining eggplant, tomato sauce, and ricotta mixture, divided in half. Add the leftover eggplant and pasta sheets on top. Add the rest of the tomato mixture on top.
4. After baking the dish covered with foil for 30 minutes, remove the foil and add mozzarella on top. Bake for an additional 20 minutes, or until it achieves a golden brown color. Let it stand for 10 minutes before serving, and garnish with fresh oregano.

Orange Glazed Salmon

PREP TIME: 5 min
COOK TIME: 20 min
TOTAL TIME: 25 min
SERVES: 4

NUTRITIONAL FACTS
Calories: 361; Fat: 18g; Carbs: 14g; Protein: 35g; Sugars: 12g; Fiber: 1g

INGREDIENTS

- 2 tablespoons of avocado oil
- 4 (6-ounce) of salmon fillets
- 1 orange, juiced
- 2 minced garlic cloves
- 2 tablespoons of honey
- 2 tablespoons of tamari
- 1 teaspoon of thyme, finely chopped
- salt, and pepper, to taste
- ½ teaspoon of arrowroot flour
- 1 teaspoon of water

DIRECTIONS

1. Apply salt and pepper to the salmon after patting it dry with a paper towel.
2. In a pan, warm the avocado oil over medium-high heat. Pan-fry the fish for 3 to 4 minutes on each side or until golden brown and cooked through
3. Make an arrowroot slurry by combining arrowroot powder and water while the salmon is cooking. Place aside.
4. Transfer the cooked fish to a platter.
5. For 30 seconds, sauté the minced garlic in the skillet over medium-low heat. Add the arrowroot slurry, honey, tamari, thyme, and orange juice. The mixture needs to slightly thicken after being whisked for one to two minutes.
6. Before serving, return the salmon to the pan and spread the glaze over it.

Notes: To prevent the salmon from sticking to the pan, I advise using a seasoned cast iron pan.
Throughout the cooling period, the glaze will continue to thicken naturally.

Ratatouille

PREP TIME: 20 min
COOK TIME: 1h
TOTAL TIME: 1 h 20 min
SERVES: 6-8

NUTRITIONAL FACTS
Calories: 230; Fat: 11g;
Carbs: 32g; Protein: 5g;
Sugars: 16g; Fiber: 8g

INGREDIENTS

- 2 eggplants
- 6 Roma tomatoes
- 2 yellow mushrooms
- 2 zucchinis

Sauce
- 2 tablespoons of olive oil
- 1 onion, chopped
- 4 minced garlic cloves
- 1 red bell pepper, diced
- 1 yellow bell pepper, diced
- salt and pepper, to taste
- 28 oz can of crushed tomatoes (795 g)
- 2 tablespoons of chopped fresh basil, 8–10 leaves

Herb Seasoning
- 2 tablespoons of chopped fresh basil, 8–10 leaves
- 1 teaspoon of garlic, minced
- 2 tablespoons of chopped fresh parsley
- 2 teaspoons of fresh thyme
- salt, to taste
- pepper, to taste
- 4 tablespoons of olive oil

DIRECTIONS

1. Set the oven's temperature to 375 °F.
2. Set aside after cutting the squash, zucchinis, tomatoes, and eggplants into rounds that are about 1/16 of an inch (1 mm) thick.
3. Create the sauce In a 12-inch (30-cm) oven-safe pan, heat the olive oil over medium-high heat. For about 10 minutes, sauté the bell peppers, onion, and garlic until tender. Add the tomatoes, then season with salt and pepper. Mix everything up thoroughly by stirring. Add the basil after turning the heat off. Repeat the stirring, then use a spatula to smooth the sauce's top.
4. From the outer edge to the center of the pan, alternately arrange the sliced vegetables (such as eggplant, tomato, squash, and zucchini) on top of the sauce. Season with salt and pepper to your preference.
5. To prepare the herb seasoning: Combine the basil, garlic, parsley, thyme, salt, pepper, and olive oil in a small bowl. Sprinkle the vegetables with the herb seasoning.
6. Bake the pan for 40 minutes with the foil covering it. Bake for an additional 20 minutes with the lid off, or until the veggies are tender.
7. Serve hot as a main course or side dish. The ratatouille is also delicious the next day; simply reheat in the microwave to the desired temperature or cover with foil and warm in a 350 °F (180 °C) oven for 15 minutes.

Baked Tilapia with Pecan Rosemary Topping

PREP TIME: 15 min
COOK TIME: 18 min
TOTAL TIME: 33 min
SERVES: 4

NUTRITIONAL FACTS
Calories: 222; Fat: 10.8g;
Carbs: 6.7g; Protein: 26.8g;
Sugars: 0.4g; Fiber: 1.6g

INGREDIENTS

- 1/3 cup finely chopped raw pecans
- 1/3 cup panko whole wheat breadcrumbs
- 2 teaspoons of chopped fresh rosemary
- ½ teaspoon of coconut palm sugar or brown sugar
- ⅛ teaspoon of salt
- 1 pinch of cayenne pepper
- 1 ½ teaspoons of olive oil
- 1 egg white
- 4 tilapia fillets (4 ounces each)

DIRECTIONS

1. Set the oven to 350 °F.
2. Pecans, breadcrumbs, rosemary, coconut palm sugar, salt, and cayenne pepper should all be combined in a small baking dish. Toss the pecan mixture with the olive oil after adding it.
3. Bake for 7 to 8 minutes, or until the pecan mixture is pale golden brown.
4. Turn up the heat to 400 °F. Spray cooking spray in a big glass baking dish.
5. The egg white should be whisked in a small dish. One tilapia at a time, lightly coat both sides of the fish by dipping it in the egg white and then the pecan mixture. Put the fillets in the baking pan that has been prepared.
6. The tops of the tilapia fillets should be pressed with the leftover pecan mixture.
7. Bake for about 10 minutes, or until the tilapia is barely cooked through. Serve.

Spanish Chicken Stew

PREP TIME: 10 min
COOK TIME: 20 min
TOTAL TIME: 30 min
SERVES: 4

NUTRITIONAL FACTS
Calories: 325; Fat: 17g;
Carbs: 7g; Protein: 35g;
Sugars: 3g; Fiber: 2g

INGREDIENTS

- ½ chicken (1/2 of a 4 pound chicken), cut into 2 pieces or 1.5 pounds boneless chicken thighs, cut into 2 pieces
- salt and pepper
- 2 tablespoons of Extra virgin olive oil
- 1 minced tiny red onion
- 1 red bell pepper, thinly sliced
- 1 minced garlic clove
- 1 can of crushed tomatoes, 15 ounces
- 1 cup of chicken broth
- 1 cup of water
- 2 bay leaves
- 1 tablespoon of oregano
- ½ cup of green olives, pitted
- 2 tablespoons of capers, chopped if too big
- ¼ cup of fresh parsley

DIRECTIONS

1. Sprinkle some salt and pepper on the chicken.
2. Heat a Dutch oven or a deep pot and add the olive oil.
3. Add the chicken and cook it until golden brown on all sides. Take out and set aside.
4. Bay leaves, oregano, water, chicken broth, and smashed tomatoes should all be added. Overheat it.
5. Re-add the chicken to the pot, making sure it's submerged in liquid up to a boil.
6. Serve the chicken with capers, green olives, and fresh parsley after simmering for another 15 minutes, or until the chicken is done.

Balsamic Glazed Roasted Vegetables

PREP TIME: 15 min
COOK TIME: 1h
TOTAL TIME: 1 h 15 min
SERVES: 4

NUTRITIONAL FACTS
Calories: 221; Fat: 10g; Carbs: 28g; Protein: 4.1g; Sugars: 6g; Fiber: 5.9g

INGREDIENTS

- 1 garlic clove cut in half
- 1 medium eggplant, cut roughly
- 3 medium zucchini, cut roughly
- 1 coarsely chopped red bell pepper
- 1 green bell pepper, chopped roughly
- 2 roughly sliced carrots
- 1 pound (450 grams) of baby potatoes cut in half
- 1 red onion, sliced
- 2 bay leaves
- 1 teaspoon of ground cumin
- 2 teaspoons of thyme
- salt and pepper to taste
- 4 tablespoons of olive oil

For the honey-balsamic glaze:
- ¼ cup of balsamic vinegar
- 3 tablespoons of honey or maple syrup for vegans

DIRECTIONS

1. Turn up the oven to 390 °F.
2. Roast the vegetables: coat a large pan or casserole dish with the garlic clove by rubbing it over the surface. Add the potatoes, onion, carrots, eggplant, and zucchini to the pan. If you prefer very soft peppers, add them now; otherwise, add them after 30 minutes. Mix thoroughly after adding the olive oil, cumin, thyme, and bay leaves. Season with salt and pepper to your preference. For 30 minutes, bake. Add the peppers, stir thoroughly, and bake for an additional 15 minutes.
3. To make the balsamic glaze, combine the honey (or maple syrup) and balsamic vinegar in a jar and shake vigorously. After thoroughly mixing, pour over the vegetables and bake for a further 15 minutes, or until thickened. The cooking time will vary based on how densely packed the pan is.

Notes: 1. For grilling the vegetables, cut baby potatoes in half lengthwise and boil until tender. Slice the remaining vegetables and brush with balsamic sauce twice while grilling. This dish pairs well with Israeli couscous.
2. Use fresh eggplant, as they become more bitter with age. Male eggplants are typically less bitter than females.

Mediterranean-Style Grilled Zucchini Salad

PREP TIME: 5 min
COOK TIME: 10 min
TOTAL TIME: 15 min
SERVES: 4

NUTRITIONAL FACTS
Calories: 176; Fat: 15g; Carbs: 8g; Protein: 5g; Sugars: 5g; Fiber: 2g

INGREDIENTS

- 4 zucchinis squash about 2 lb, sliced into rounds
- 1 tablespoon of olive oil
- 1 teaspoon of organic ground cumin
- juice of 1 lemon
- 1 minced garlic clove
- salt and pepper
- 1 cup of packed chopped fresh parsley
- 2 teaspoons of chopped fresh tarragon
- feta or goat cheese (optional)

DIRECTIONS

1. Toss a large bowl of sliced zucchinis with extra virgin olive oil and cumin. Grill or griddle for 4 minutes in batches until cooked and charred.
2. Return to the bowl and add lemon juice, garlic, salt, pepper and fresh herbs.
3. Toss again. Serve on a platter and garnish with feta or goat cheese, if desired.

Shrimp Tacos with Best Shrimp Taco Sauce

PREP TIME: 25 min
COOK TIME: 5 min
TOTAL TIME: 30 min
SERVES: 4

NUTRITIONAL FACTS
Calories: 308; Fat: 18g;
Carbs: 21g; Protein: 17g;
Sugars: 4g; Fiber: 5g

INGREDIENTS

For the Shrimps:
Shrimps
- 1-pound shrimps (medium or large)
- 1 minced or pressed garlic clove
- ½ teaspoon of sea salt
- ¼ teaspoon of black pepper
- ¼ teaspoon of ground cumin
- ¼ teaspoon of cayenne pepper
- 1 tablespoon of olive oil

Shrimp Taco Toppings
- 8 white corn tortillas, (small, 6" diameter), or Hard Taco Shells
- ½ small purple cabbage, 2 cups shredded
- 1 large pitted, peeled, and chopped avocado
- ½ red onion, chopped
- 4 oz Cotija cheese, (1 cup grated on a box grater)
- ¼ bunch of chopped cilantro
- 1 lime, cut into 8 wedges

Shrimp Taco Sauce Ingredients
- 30 ml of sour cream
- 30 ml of mayonnaise
- 1 medium lime, squeezed into 1 ½ tablespoons of lime juice
- ¾ teaspoon of garlic powder
- ¾ teaspoon of Sriracha sauce, or to taste

DIRECTIONS

1. Thaw the shrimps and dry them with paper towels. Add them to a medium bowl and mix in the seasoning and garlic.
2. Heat a large non-stick pan over medium-high heat and add 1 tbsp of olive oil. Once hot, add the shrimps in a single layer and sauté for 1–2 minutes per side, or until cooked through. Once cooked, transfer them to a serving platter and let them cool
3. Char 8 tortillas over a medium/low flame on a gas stove top for about 10 seconds per side, or until slightly charred on the edges. Alternatively, you can also toast them on a medium-hot skillet or griddle for 30 seconds per side until golden brown in some spots.
4. Slice the cabbage thinly, dice the avocado, mince the red onion, and roughly chop the cilantro. Arrange these ingredients, along with lime wedges, on a serving platter. Place the toppings and shrimps on each toasted tortilla before assembling the tacos.
5. In a separate small bowl, combine the ingredients for the sauce and serve it alongside the assembled shrimp tacos.

Crispy Sheet Pan Salmon with Lemony Asparagus and Carrots

PREP TIME: 20 min
COOK TIME: 20 min
TOTAL TIME: 40 min
SERVES: 4

NUTRITIONAL FACTS
Calories: 230; Fat: 12.5g;
Carbs: 4.4g; Protein: 27.8g;
Sugars: 2.1g; Fiber: 2.4g

INGREDIENTS

- 4 salmon fillets, each weighing 6 ounces
- ¼ cup of mayonnaise
- 2 tablespoons of Dijon mustard
- 1 tablespoon of freshly chopped dill
- 1 ½ teaspoons of lemon zest (from 1 lemon), divided
- ¾ teaspoon of kosher salt, divided
- ¾ teaspoon of black pepper, divided
- ¼ cup of panko (Japanese-style breadcrumbs)
- cooking spray
- ½ pound of fresh asparagus, trimmed
- 1 (8-oz.) package of tiny carrots with tops, cut lengthwise
- 2 tablespoons of melted unsalted butter
- slice of lemon

DIRECTIONS

1. Set the oven to 425°F and line a baking sheet with parchment paper. Place the salmon, skin side down, on half of the prepared sheet. Mix mayonnaise, mustard, dill, 1 tsp of lemon zest, 1/4 tsp of salt, and 1/4 tsp of pepper in a bowl. Spread the mixture over the salmon fillets evenly. Sprinkle panko on top and press it down lightly. Spray with cooking spray
2. Mix asparagus, carrots, butter, and the remaining ½ tsp of lemon zest, salt, and pepper in a bowl. Place the vegetables on the other half of the baking sheet. Cook in the oven until the salmon is cooked, and the vegetables are tender, around 18 minutes. Serve with lemon wedges.

Buffalo Chicken Zucchini Boats

PREP TIME: 10 min
COOK TIME: 35 min
TOTAL TIME: 45 min
SERVES: 4

NUTRITIONAL FACTS
Calories: 515; Fat: 22.6g;
Carbs: 5.9g; Protein: 39.7g;
Sugars: 0.9g; Fiber: 0.5g

INGREDIENTS

- 4 medium zucchinis, cut lengthwise in half (try to find zucchinis that are similar in size)
- 1 ½ pounds of rotisserie chicken or shredded chicken breast
- 1 cup of vegan mayo
- 1 cup of coconut cream (full fat from the can)
- 1 teaspoon of garlic powder
- 1 teaspoon of dried dill
- 1 ½ teaspoons of dried chives
- 1 teaspoon of paprika
- 1 tablespoon of lemon juice
- ¾ cup of hot sauce (if you want it to be less spicy, use less)

DIRECTIONS

1. Grease a big baking pan with foil and preheat the oven to 400 °F. Place aside.
2. Each zucchini half should have its core hollowed out using a big spoon, leaving a rim of about 1/2 inch to serve as boats. On the large baking sheet that has been lined with foil, arrange the hollowed-out zucchini. Place aside.
3. In a medium bowl, mix together the shredded chicken, mayo, coconut cream, garlic powder, dill, chives, paprika, lemon juice, and spicy sauce.
4. Fill the zucchini boats evenly with the buffalo chicken mixture, and bake for 35 minutes, or until the zucchini are soft, and the buffalo chicken is just starting to brown on top.
5. Add fresh chives, parsley, or scallions, a paleo-friendly ranch (we like Tessamae's), or both to the top.

Notes: Greek yogurt can be used in place of the coconut cream if you are not dairy-free.

Vegetarian Stuffed Grape Leaves

PREP TIME: 50 min
COOK TIME: 1 h 10 min
TOTAL TIME: 2 h min
SERVES: 8

NUTRITIONAL FACTS
Calories: 209; Fat: 4g;
Carbs: 47g; Protein: 4g;
Sugars: 2g; Fiber: 4g

INGREDIENTS

- 2 glasses of warm water
- 1 cup of medium-grain white rice, uncooked
- 5 teaspoons kosher salt
- 6 tablespoons olive oil
- 4 large onions, cut finely (about 8 1/2 cups)
- 1 large bunch of fresh flat-leaf parsley, finely chopped (about 1 cup)
- 1 big bunch of freshly cut dill (about 1 cup)
- 2 teaspoons of dried mint (such as Burlap & Barrel)
- 2 teaspoons of granulated sugar
- ¼ teaspoon of black pepper
- 45 jarred brined grape leaves, rinsed
- 2 glasses of water
- 2 tablespoons of fresh lemon juice

DIRECTIONS

1. Mix 2 cups of warm water, rice, and 1 teaspoon of salt in a medium bowl and let sit for 20 minutes. Rinse and drain the rice.
2. In a large skillet over medium high heat, add ¼ cup of oil. Once hot, add onions and cook, stirring frequently, until they are softened, which should take about 20 minutes. Next, add the drained rice and cook, still stirring frequently, for 5 minutes. After that, add parsley, dill, dried mint, sugar, black pepper, and the remaining 4 teaspoons of salt. Cook and stir for an additional minute, then remove the skillet from heat.
3. Take 1 grape leaf and lay it out on a work surface with the veins facing up. Put 1 heaping tbsp of the rice mixture in the center of the leaf. Fold the stem end up around the filling and then fold in the sides, roll the grape leaf up until the filling is completely encased. Repeat this process with the remaining grape leaves and filling.
4. Arrange the stuffed grape leaves in a single layer at the bottom of a 12-inch saucepan. Put any remaining stuffed leaves on top. Pour 2 cups of water, lemon juice, and the remaining 2 tablespoons of oil over the top. Cover the pan with a heatproof plate (do not use the pan lid) and cook over medium heat for 5 minutes. Lower the heat to low and put the pan lid over the plate, continue to cook for 40 minutes. Once done, remove the pan from heat. Remove the lid and plate and let it stand for 10 minutes

Notes: You can store stuffed grape leaves in the fridge for an entire night. Before serving, bring to room temperature.

Vegetarian Stuffed Eggplant

PREP TIME: 20 min
COOK TIME: 45 min
TOTAL TIME: 1 h 5 min
SERVES: 4

NUTRITIONAL FACTS
Calories: 255; Fat: 1.6g;
Carbs: 44g; Protein: 10g;
Sugars: 4g; Fiber: 11g

INGREDIENTS

- 2 big eggplants
- ¼ teaspoon of kosher salt
- 1 tablespoon Extra virgin olive oil

Spice mixture:
- ¾ teaspoon of allspice
- ¾ teaspoon of coriander
- ½ teaspoon of paprika
- ½ teaspoon of ground cinnamon

Filling:
- 1 cup of dried couscous
- 1 cup canned or cooked chickpeas drained
- 1 sliced tiny Roma tomato
- 1 chopped green onion
- a handful of chopped, fresh parsley

To Serve:
- Tahini sauce made in accordance with this recipe

DIRECTIONS

1. Cut the eggplants in half lengthwise. Season the flesh with kosher salt and set it aside with the flesh side up for 20 to 30 minutes. This will make the eggplant «sweat.» (This is an optional step, but it can make a big difference). After that, pat the eggplant dry using a paper towel.
2. Preheat the oven to 425 °F.
3. Mix together allspice, coriander, paprika and ground cinnamon in a small bowl
4. Dry the eggplant with a paper towel. Brush the flesh with extra virgin olive oil. Reserve 1 teaspoon of the spice mixture and use the rest to season the eggplant by rubbing the mixture all over the flesh.
5. Roast the eggplants by placing the halves, flesh side up, on a well-oiled sheet pan. Bake in the preheated oven for 35–45 minutes, or until the flesh is tender
6. As the eggplant is roasting, prepare the instant couscous. Heat a small amount of extra virgin olive oil in a saucepan. Add the couscous and cook, stirring frequently, until it is toasted. Add 1 cup of boiling water to the couscous and remove the pan from heat. Cover the pan and let it sit for 10 minutes, or until the couscous is cooked (it will double in size).
7. Make the filling by fluffing the couscous with a fork and seasoning it with a dash of salt and the 1 teaspoon of spice mixture you reserved earlier. Add chickpeas, chopped tomatoes, green onions, and parsley and toss everything together to combine
8. Assemble the stuffed eggplant by placing the roasted eggplant halves on a serving platter, flesh side up. Use the back of a spoon to press down on the flesh to create a space for the couscous filling. Fill the space with the couscous mixture. Drizzle tahini sauce over the top if desired. Serve and enjoy!

Notes:
1. *Pro-tip:* Salting the eggplant before roasting is a recommended step, as it removes bitterness and improves texture.
2. *For a gluten-free option:* Substitute the couscous with cooked quinoa.
3. *Prep Ahead:* You can roast the eggplant a day before and store it in a covered container in the fridge. Remember to bring it to room temperature before adding the filling.
4. *Storage*: The stuffed eggplant is best enjoyed fresh, but can be stored in the fridge for 2 to 3 days.

Spicy Chicken and Sweet Potato Stew

PREP TIME: 25 min
COOK TIME: 25 min
TOTAL TIME: 50 min
SERVES: 6

NUTRITIONAL FACTS
Calories: 361; Fat: 8g;
Carbs: 44g; Protein: 29g;
Sugars: 5g; Fiber: 7g

INGREDIENTS

- ½ chicken (1/2 of a 4 1 teaspoon of olive oil
- 1 onion, chopped
- 4 cloves of garlic, minced
- 1 pound of sweet potatoes, peeled and cubed
- 1 orange bell pepper, seeded and cubed
- 1 pound of cooked chicken breast, cubed
- 1 (28 ounces) can dice tomatoes
- 2 cups of water
- 1 teaspoon of salt
- 2 tablespoons of chili powder
- 1 teaspoon of ground cumin
- 1 teaspoon of dried oregano
- 1 teaspoon of cocoa powder
- ¼ teaspoon of ground cinnamon
- ¼ teaspoon of red pepper flakes
- 1 ½ tablespoons of all-purpose flour
- 2 tbsp of water
- 1 cup of frozen corn
- 1 (16-ounce) can of kidney beans, rinsed and drained
- ½ cup chopped fresh cilantro

DIRECTIONS

1. Heat olive oil in a pot over medium heat. Add onion and garlic and cook, stirring occasionally, until the onion is translucent. Then, mix in the sweet potatoes, bell pepper, chicken, tomatoes, and 2 cups of water. Season with salt, chili powder, cumin, oregano, cocoa powder, cinnamon, and red pepper flakes. Bring the mixture to a boil, then reduce the heat and simmer for 10–20 minutes or until the potatoes are tender, stirring occasionally to prevent sticking.

2. Once done, add the corn and kidney beans and cook until heated through. Lastly, stir in the cilantro before serving.

Cooked Octopus Tentacles with Chorizo and Potatoes

PREP TIME: 20 min
COOK TIME: 25 min
TOTAL TIME: 45 min
SERVES: 4

NUTRITIONAL FACTS
Calories: 274; Fat: 6.9g;
Carbs: 18.3g; Protein: 32.6g;
Sugars: 3g; Fiber: 3.9g

INGREDIENTS

- 1 pack of cooked octopus tentacles
- 340 g potatoes, peeled and diced
- sea salt
- ground pepper
- 3 tablespoons of Extra-virgin olive oil, plus more for drizzling
- 2 teaspoons of chopped thyme
- 140 g sliced cured Spanish chorizo

DIRECTIONS

1. Dice the octopus tentacles and set them aside.
2. In a separate saucepan, boil the potatoes (seasoned with salt) until tender. Drain and transfer to a bowl.
3. Mix the cooked potatoes with 3 tablespoons of extra-virgin olive oil, thyme, salt, and pepper
4. Begin by grilling the chorizo over high heat in a grill pan for 2 minutes, or until heated through. Remove from the pan and transfer to a bowl.
5. Then, add the potatoes and octopus to the same pan and cook until golden and hot, about 5 minutes. Add to the bowl with the chorizo, season with salt and pepper, and toss.
6. Drizzle with extra virgin olive oil and serve

Instant Pot Harissa Bean Stew

PREP TIME: 20 min
COOK TIME: 40 min
TOTAL TIME: 1 h
SERVES: 6

NUTRITIONAL FACTS
Calories: 269; Fat: 19g;
Carbs: 21g; Protein: 8g;
Sugars: 4g; Fiber: 14g

INGREDIENTS

- ½ cup of vegetable oil
- 6 minced garlic cloves
- 2 tablespoons of smoked paprika
- 1 tablespoon of ground coriander
- 1 tablespoon of ground cumin
- 1 teaspoon of ground caraway
- 1 teaspoon of kosher salt
- ½ to 1 teaspoon of cayenne pepper

Bean Stew
- 1½ cups of soaked and drained dried 15-bean mixture
- 1 cup of canned diced tomatoes
- 1 cup of chopped carrots
- 1 cup of chopped onion
- 1 cup of chopped celery
- 1 to 2 tbsp of harissa
- 1 teaspoon of ground turmeric
- 1 teaspoon of kosher salt
- ½ teaspoon of black pepper
- 2½ cups of water
- 2 tablespoons of apple cider vinegar
- ½ cup of chopped fresh parsley

DIRECTIONS

1. Harissa: Combine the oil, garlic, paprika, coriander, cumin, caraway, salt, and cayenne pepper in a medium microwave-safe bowl. 1 minute on high in the microwave, stirring once halfway through. Until the oil is heated and boiling, you can also cook this on the stove top.
2. Allow it to cool completely. For up to a month, keep in the refrigerator in an airtight container.
3. Stew: Place the bean mixture, tomatoes, carrots, onion, celery, harissa, turmeric, salt, pepper, and water in the Instant Pot.
4. Put the pot's lid on securely. Close the valve that releases pressure. Choose Manual, then set the pressure cooker to High for 30 minutes. After the cooking period is through, let the pot lie idle for 10 minutes before performing a Quick-Release to let out any leftover pressure.
5. Use an immersion blender to purée the soup, or crush some of the beans with the back of a spoon to thicken it. Serve after adding the vinegar and parsley.

Air-Fryer Scallops with Lemon-Herb Sauce

PREP TIME: 10 min
COOK TIME: 10 min
TOTAL TIME: 20 min
SERVES: 2

NUTRITIONAL FACTS
Calories: 348; Fat: 30g;
Carbs: 5g; Protein: 14g;
Sugars: 3g; Fiber: 3g

INGREDIENTS

- 8 large (1oz) sea scallops, cleaned and thoroughly dried
- ¼ teaspoon of ground pepper
- ⅛ teaspoon of salt
- cooking spray
- ¼ cup of Extra-virgin olive oil
- 2 tablespoons of very finely chopped flat-leaf parsley
- 2 teaspoons of capers, very finely chopped
- 1 teaspoon of finely grated lemon zest
- ½ teaspoon of finely chopped garlic
- lemon wedges, optional

DIRECTIONS

1. Season the scallops with pepper and salt. Spray the basket of an air fryer with cooking spray, then place the scallops in the basket and spray them with additional cooking oil. Put the basket in the fryer and cook the scallops at 400°F until they reach an internal temperature of 120°F, which should take about 6 minutes.
2. In a small bowl, mix together oil, parsley, capers, lemon zest, and garlic. Drizzle this mixture over the cooked scallops. Lemon wedges should be served, if desired.

Wolfgang Puck's Tomato Risotto With Shrimps

PREP TIME: 10 min
COOK TIME: 25 min
TOTAL TIME: 35 min
SERVES: 2

NUTRITIONAL FACTS
Calories: 871; Fat: 68g;
Carbs: 73g; Protein: 12g;
Sugars: 9g; Fiber: 2g

INGREDIENTS

- 6 tablespoons of olive oil, divided
- 2 teaspoons of minced garlic
- 1 tablespoon of minced shallot
- 1 cup of arborio rice (230 g)
- ¼ cup of dry white wine (60 g)
- 2 cups of chicken stock (480 g), boiling
- 14.5 oz tomato soup (410 g), 1 can
- 6 tablespoons of unsalted butter, cubed
- ¼ cup of Parmesan cheese (30 g), freshly grated
- kosher salt, to taste
- ground white pepper, to taste
- 8 large shrimps that have been peeled, deveined, and butterflied
- ¼ cup of green peas (40 g)
- 1 tablespoon of minced fresh parsley leaves for a garnish

DIRECTIONS

1. Start by heating 3 tablespoons of olive oil in a medium skillet over medium heat. Add in shallots and 1 teaspoon of minced garlic, sautéing until soft.
2. Toss in the rice and stir until it's well coated with the oil. Deglaze the pan with wine, allowing it to reduce until the pan is almost dry.
3. Using a ladle, add one ladle of boiling stock to the rice at a time, stirring until the stock is absorbed, and the rice is almost dry. Continue this process until the rice is tender, but still firm, resulting in a moist and creamy texture.
4. Stir in the tomato basil bisque and remove from heat. Fold in butter and Parmesan cheese, seasoning with salt and pepper.
5. In another skillet, heat the remaining 3 tablespoons of olive oil over medium heat. Add the remaining teaspoon of minced garlic, shrimp, salt, white pepper and peas. Cook until the shrimp is pink and opaque, about 4–5 minutes.
6. Remove from heat and sprinkle with parsley. Serve the risotto on 2 plates and top each with half the shrimp and peas. Enjoy!

Baked Chicken and Ricotta Meatballs

PREP TIME: 15 min
COOK TIME: 15 min
TOTAL TIME: 30 min
SERVES: 4

NUTRITIONAL FACTS
Calories: 454; Fat: 27g;
Carbs: 20g; Protein: 38g;
Sugars: 3g; Fiber: 7g

INGREDIENTS

- 14 ounces (400g) of broccolini, with the thick portions sliced lengthwise and the tough stems removed
- 1 lemon, finely sliced after trimming the end
- 4 tablespoons of Extra-virgin olive oil, divided
- kosher salt and freshly ground black pepper
- ½ teaspoon of red pepper flakes, or more if you like
- 1 big egg
- 2 garlic cloves, grated
- ¾ cup ricotta cheese, drained and moderately salted
- ½ cup of parsley leaves and fine stems, roughly chopped
- ¾ cup panko breadcrumbs
- 1 pound of ground chicken, preferably dark meat
- 1 lemon (juice)
- grated Parmesan, for sprinkling (optional)

DIRECTIONS

1. Begin by preheating the oven to 425°F.
2. On a baking sheet, combine the broccoli and lemon slices with 3 tablespoons of olive oil, salt, pepper, and red pepper flakes. Mix well and spread the mixture evenly on the baking sheet. Keep the baking sheet aside while you prepare the meatballs.
3. *Prepare the meatballs:* In a medium bowl, whisk the egg, then add the garlic, ricotta, 1 teaspoon of salt, parsley, pepper, remaining oil, breadcrumbs, and meat. Gently mix everything together using your hands (over-mixing will make the meatballs tough and dry). The meat should be visible in small chunks. Form 20 small meatballs by moistening your hands with water or oil and rolling the meat mixture. Make sure to use a gentle rolling motion while shaping them. Place the meatballs on large pieces of baking parchment on the counter for easy cleanup.
4. Place the meatballs on a baking sheet with broccoli and lemon, and bake in the oven for 15–20 minutes. After removing from the oven, the dish is finished with a squeeze of lemon juice and grated Parmesan cheese before serving.

Greek Chicken Kabobs

PREP TIME: 30 min
COOK TIME: 25 min
TOTAL TIME: 55 min
SERVES: 6

NUTRITIONAL FACTS
Calories: 135; Fat: 6g;
Carbs: 11g; Protein: 10g;
Sugars: 4g; Fiber: 3g

INGREDIENTS

Marinade
- ¼ cup of olive oil
- 2 tablespoons of red wine vinegar
- 3 tablespoons of lemon juice
- 1 teaspoon of Dijon mustard
- 3 minced garlic cloves
- 1 teaspoon of dried oregano
- ½ teaspoon of salt
- ¼ teaspoon of black pepper

Chicken Kabobs
- 3 large boneless, skinless chicken breasts weighing 1 ½ pounds each, cut into 1 ½ -inch chunk.
- 1 red bell pepper, cut into 1 ½ -Inch chunks after seeding it
- 1 yellow bell pepper, cut into 1 ½ -inch slices after seeding it
- 1 red onion, diced into 1 ½ -inch pieces
- 1 zucchini, sliced

DIRECTIONS

1. Create a flavorful marinade by whisking together olive oil, red wine vinegar, lemon juice, Dijon mustard, minced garlic, dried oregano, salt, and pepper.
2. Coat the chicken in the marinade and let it sit in the fridge for at least an hour to allow the flavors to penetrate.
3. When ready to cook, preheat the grill to medium-high heat. Thread chicken, red onion, zucchini, and bell pepper onto skewers in any order you prefer.
4. Grill the kabobs for about 5–7 minutes per side or until the chicken is cooked through, and the vegetables are lightly charred, around 15 minutes.
5. Serve with a squeeze of lemon wedges and a side of tzatziki sauce for an extra burst of flavor.
Notes:
   1. Keep leftovers fresh by storing them in an airtight container and refrigerating for up to 3 days.
   2. For longer storage, freeze your kabobs in a freezer-safe bag or container for up to 3 months.
   3. When ready to enjoy your kabobs again, simply

Roasted Cabbage Steaks

PREP TIME: 10 min
COOK TIME: 25 min
TOTAL TIME: 35 min
SERVES: 4

NUTRITIONAL FACTS
Calories: 200; Fat: 11g;
Carbs: 24g; Protein: 5g;
Sugars: 6g; Fiber: 9g

INGREDIENTS

- 2 small cabbage heads
- 3 tablespoons of Extra virgin olive oil
- ½ teaspoon of salt or to taste
- 2 teaspoons of paprika
- 1 tablespoon of garlic powder

DIRECTIONS

1. Remove the stems from the cabbage heads and cut them into quarters by slicing each one in half, then in half again. Each head should yield four pieces of cabbage that are about ¾ to 1 inch thick. Arrange the cabbage steaks on a baking sheet lined with parchment paper, making sure to leave some space between them for even cooking.
2. Coat the cabbage steaks thoroughly with olive oil using a brush. Sprinkle a generous amount of salt, garlic powder, and paprika on one side of the cabbage. Flip the cabbage over and repeat the process on the other side. Add a pinch of red pepper flakes to each steak, if desired.
3. Place the cabbage steaks in the oven and bake at 400 °F for approximately 25 minutes, or until the leaves are browned and the center is tender. Serve immediately after baking.
Notes:
   This Cabbage Curry can be paired in many ways: serve it with your favorite pasta and sauce for a classic pairing, combine it with other grains such as quinoa, bulgur, millet, barley, farro, or wheat. Try it with other vegetables like riced cauliflower, roasted eggplant, or sautéed mushrooms for a delicious and healthy combination.

CHAPTER 4
SALAT RECIPES

Fig Salad with Parma Ham & Blue Cheese

PREP TIME: 5 min
COOK TIME: 5 min
TOTAL TIME: 10 min
SERVES: 1-2

NUTRITIONAL FACTS
Calories: 207; Fat: 14g;
Carbs: 13.6g; Protein: 8.5g;
Sugars: 9.2g; Fiber: 2.3g

INGREDIENTS

- 4 washed and quartered figs
- 4 slices of Parma ham
- 60g (2oz) dolcelatte, or blue cheese
- 2 tablespoons chopped basil leaves
- 2 tablespoons Extra virgin olive oil
- salt and pepper, to taste

DIRECTIONS

1. Four dishes should include figs, ham, and cheese on each.
2. Basil leaves should be added along with some oil.
3. Serve right away after seasoning to taste. Enjoy!

Notes:
For this recipe, blue cheeses like Stilton, Roquefort, Cambozola, Cashel blue, Danish blue cheese, dolcelatte, and Gorgonzola will work well.

Fig & Goat Cheese Salad

PREP TIME: 5 min
COOK TIME: 5 min
TOTAL TIME: 10 min
SERVES: 1-2

NUTRITIONAL FACTS
Calories: 340; Fat: 21g;
Carbs: 31.8g; Protein: 10.4g;
Sugars: 18g; Fiber: 7g

INGREDIENTS

- 2 cups mixed salad greens
- 4 sliced and stemmed dried figs
- 1 ounce of fresh goat cheese, crumbled
- 1½ tablespoons of slivered almonds, preferably toasted
- 2 tablespoons of Extra-virgin olive oil
- 2 tablespoons of balsamic vinegar
- ½ teaspoon of honey
- pinch of salt
- freshly ground pepper to taste

DIRECTIONS

1. In the first step, mix the greens, figs, goat cheese, and almonds in a bowl. Combine oil, vinegar, honey, salt, and pepper in a bowl.
2. Drizzle the salad with the dressing just before serving, and toss.

Notes:
Making ahead: Salad and dressing can both be kept in the refrigerator for up to 24 hours.

Pumpkin and Chickpea Salad with Sun-Dried Tomatoes and Feta

PREP TIME: 10 min
COOK TIME: 40 min
TOTAL TIME: 50 min
SERVES: 6-8

NUTRITIONAL FACTS
Calories: 149; Fat: 5.9g; Carbs: 20g; Protein: 5.5g; Sugars: 6g; Fiber: 4.7g

INGREDIENTS

- ½ medium pumpkin (roughly 2 cups)
- 1 can (400gm/15oz) of chickpeas, drained and rinsed
- ½ red onion
- ½ cup of sun-dried tomatoes
- ½ cup of goat feta, cut into cubes
- ½ cup of fresh mint
- salt and pepper to taste

Salad dressing:

- 2 tablespoon of Extra virgin olive oil
- 1 tablespoon of balsamic vinegar
- 1 garlic clove, peeled and minced

DIRECTIONS

1. Set the oven to 355 °F.
2. The pumpkin should be peeled and sliced into big chunks. When the pumpkin is ready, place it in a roasting pan and roast it in the oven for 35 to 40 minutes.
3. Take the pumpkin out of the oven and let it cool.
4. Cut the sun-dried tomatoes, fresh mint, and red onion into small dice.
5. In a sizable salad bowl, combine the pumpkin, chickpeas, sun-dried tomatoes, mint, and goat feta.
6. Just before serving, drizzle the dressing over the pumpkin salad.

Notes:
1. For the feta in this pumpkin salad, I used goat's milk cheese. If you'd rather, you may substitute it with vegan feta or another type of cheese.
2. In a refrigerator airtight container, this pumpkin and chickpea salad should keep for up to three days.
3. This will serve as a side dish for 6–8 people, and the nutritional data is based on serving 6.

Strawberry Avocado Spinach Salad with Poppy Seed Dressing

PREP TIME: 10 min
COOK TIME: 5 min
TOTAL TIME: 15 min
SERVES: 4-6

NUTRITIONAL FACTS
Calories: 218; Fat: 16g; Carbs: 13g; Protein: 4g; Sugars: 7g; Fiber: 5g

INGREDIENTS

- 6 cups of fresh baby spinach
- 1 pint sliced and hulled strawberries
- 1 avocado, chopped after being pitted.
- 4 ounces of crumbled blue cheese (or goat cheese or feta)
- 1/3 cup of sliced almonds, toasted
- half a small red onion, carefully sliced

Poppy Seed Dressing

- 1/3 cup of avocado oil (or olive oil)
- 3 tablespoons of red wine vinegar
- 2 tablespoons of honey
- 1 tablespoon of poppy seeds
- 1 tablespoon of Dijon mustard
- fine sea salt and freshly ground black pepper

DIRECTIONS

1. Make the dressing. Until emulsified, briskly whisk all the ingredients in a small bowl (or shake in a closed container). If necessary, give it a taste test and add a pinch of salt and some pepper.
2. Shake the salad. In a big bowl, combine all the salad ingredients. The dressing should be drizzled evenly over the salad before being gently mixed.
3. Serve. Serve right away and delight in!

Cherry Tomato and Asparagus Salad

PREP TIME: 10 min
COOK TIME: 10 min
TOTAL TIME: 20 min
SERVES: 4

NUTRITIONAL FACTS
Calories: 213; Fat: 17g;
Carbs: 13g; Protein: 5.9g;
Sugars: 4g; Fiber: 5.9g

INGREDIENTS

- 1 pound of trimmed and divided asparagus
- 6 cups of colorful cherry, grape, and pear tomatoes cut in half.
- ½ cup of Gorgonzola cheese in crumbles
- 1 ripe avocado, cut into cubes
- 1 cup of basil leaves, diced
- ¼ cup of Extra-virgin olive oil
- 2 teaspoons of lemon juice
- 2 teaspoons of Dijon mustard
- ½ teaspoon of kosher salt
- ½ teaspoon of pepper

DIRECTIONS

1. Boil asparagus for two minutes in a big pot of salted water. Rinse with cold water after draining.
2. Combine the other ingredients with the asparagus in a big dish and swirl thoroughly to cover everything with the dressing.

Tomato Peach Burrata Salad

PREP TIME: 10 min
COOK TIME: 5 min
TOTAL TIME: 15 min
SERVES: 5-6

NUTRITIONAL FACTS
Calories: 130; Fat: 10g;
Carbs: 8g; Protein: 8g;
Sugars: 6g; Fiber: 2g

INGREDIENTS

- 2 large heirloom tomatoes, sliced
- 2 to 3 ripe of peaches, sliced
- 1 ½ cups of grape or cherry tomatoes, halved
- 8 ounces of burrata cheese, drained and wiped dry
- freshly ground black pepper and kosher salt, to taste
- olive oil as a drizzle
- glazed balsamic for drizzling
- freshly chopped basil, for adornment
- grilled bread for serving (optional)

DIRECTIONS

1. On a big dish, arrange the sliced tomatoes, peaches, and grape tomatoes. The burrata cheese ball should be broken up and placed on top of the salad. Add salt and pepper to taste.
2. Add a little balsamic and olive glaze. Fresh basil is a good garnish. If desired, serve with grilled bread.

Mixed Seafood Salad

PREP TIME: 20 min
COOK TIME: 1h 20 min
TOTAL TIME: 1h 40 min
SERVES: 6

NUTRITIONAL FACTS
Calories: 247; Fat: 7.3g;
Carbs: 5.2g; Protein: 38.8g;
Sugars: 6g; Fiber: 0.2g

INGREDIENTS

- 6 cups of water
- 1 teaspoon of salt
- ½ pound of cleaned squid
- ½ pound of medium shrimps, peeled and deveined
- ½ pound of bay scallops
- ½ pound of cleaned octopus
- ½ pound of cooked lobster meat, cut into 1-inch pieces (about 3 tails)
- ½ pound of drained and shell-piece-free lump crab meat
- ¼ cup of fresh lemon juice
- 3 tablespoons of chopped fresh flat-leaf parsley
- 3 tablespoons of chopped fresh chives
- 2 tablespoons of Extra virgin olive oil
- 2 garlic of cloves, minced
- lemon wedges (optional)
- parsley sprigs (optional)

DIRECTIONS

1. Using a large saucepan over medium-high heat, bring 6 cups of water and salt to a boil. Squid is added and cooked for 3 minutes, or until just soft. With a slotted spoon, remove the squid from the pan. Pour ice water over the squid, then drain. Squid should be cut into 1-inch chunks. Squid should be put in a big bowl.
2. Stir in the shrimps and simmer them for three minutes, or until done. Using a slotted spoon, take the shrimps out of the pan. Put them in ice water and then drain.
3. In the pan, place a vegetable steamer. Medium-low heat should be used. Scallops should be arranged in a steamer and cooked for 6 minutes at a simmer, or until done. Drain after dropping scallops into ice water. Cover and chill the mixture.
4. Remove the steamer from the pan. In a pot of simmering water, add the octopus. Cover and cook for 1 to 1 ½ hours, or until fork-tender (add additional water, if necessary, to cover octopus). Immerse the octopus in freezing water, then drain. Rub the skin off. Octopus should be cut into 1-inch chunks. Add lobster, crab, and octopus to the scallop mixture. Add juice and the remaining 4 ingredients (up till the garlic); gently mix to incorporate, and at least two hours to chill. Garnish with lemon wedges and parsley sprigs, if desired.

Beet Grapefruit and Feta Salad

PREP TIME: 20 min
COOK TIME: 50+20 min
TOTAL TIME: 1 h 30 min
SERVES: 4

NUTRITIONAL FACTS
Calories: 142; Fat: 11g;
Carbs: 5g; Protein: 3g;
Sugars: 7g; Fiber: 5g

INGREDIENTS

- 500 g of 6 large red beets, peeled
- freshly ground black pepper and sea salt
- 2 grapefruits, pink
- 1 container of Feta Cheese from Saputo
- 3 tablespoons of olive oil
- 2 tablespoons of honey
- 1 tablespoon of white wine vinegar
- ¼ cup of shelled pistachios, crushed
- fresh basil

DIRECTIONS

1. Set the oven's temperature to 400 F. Use aluminum foil to cover a baking sheet. Transfer the beets to the baking sheet after being peeled. Add salt and pepper, then sprinkle with olive oil. To form a bundle, assemble the aluminum foil's four corners. To the bundle, add 30 mL (2 tbsp) of water, then twist the top closed. The beets should be roasted for about 50 minutes, or until a sharp knife can be used to readily penetrate them. Open the package, allow the beets to cool for about 20 minutes until they are warm, and then cut them into cubes. Put in a large bowl
2. Mix the olive oil, honey, and vinegar in a small basin. Add salt and pepper to taste. To properly melt and incorporate the honey into the dressing, reheat it for a brief period of time in the microwave or on the stove. Warm beets should be covered with half of the dressing, which should be combined. Onto a sizable serving platter, transfer the beets.
3. Set the segmented, peeled grapefruits on top of the beets. Distribute the Saputo Feta Cheese chunks over the grapefruit and beets. Add the remaining dressing and drizzle. Serve right away after garnishing with fresh basil.

Notes: Be aware that you can use pre-cooked, ready-to-use beets in this recipe. In the supermarket's chilled produce department, you can find them vacuum-packed. The beets should only be chopped into cubes and warmed briefly (a few seconds in the microwave or a few minutes in the oven) before serving. Put the salad together as directed.

Traditional Greek Salad

PREP TIME: 10 min
COOK TIME: 5 min
TOTAL TIME: 15 min
SERVES: 6

NUTRITIONAL FACTS
Calories: 103; Fat: 9.5g;
Carbs: 4.7g; Protein: 1g;
Sugars: 3g; Fiber: 1.1g

INGREDIENTS

- 1 medium red onion
- 4 medium-sized, juicy tomatoes
- 1 cucumber, with the skin partially removed to create stripes
- 1 green bell pepper
- A handful of Greek Kalamata olives with pits, as desired
- kosher salt, a little bit
- 4 tablespoons of extra virgin olive oil
- 1–2 tablespoons of red wine vinegar
- Greek feta cheese comes in blocks; do not crumble the feta; leave it in big pieces
- ½ tablespoon dried oregano

DIRECTIONS

1. Slice the red onion into half-moon shapes after cutting it in half. To soften the bite, briefly soak the onion slices in a mix of chilled water and vinegar before adding them to the salad.
2. Slice or chop the tomatoes into big bits.
3. Slice the cucumber into thick (at least 12» thick) halves after cutting it in half lengthwise.
4. Rings of bell pepper should be thinly sliced.
5. Put everything into a sizable salad bowl. Add a few pitted Kalamata olives.
6. Just a pinch of kosher salt and some dried oregano is used to season the food.
7. Over the salad, drizzle red wine vinegar, and olive oil. Toss everything together with great care (do NOT over mix, this salad is not meant to be handled too much).
8. The feta blocks should now be added on top, along with a little extra dried oregano. Serving suggestion: crusty bread.

Balela Salad Recipe

PREP TIME: 10 min
COOK TIME: 5 min
TOTAL TIME: 15 min
SERVES: 4

NUTRITIONAL FACTS
Calories: 267; Fat: 7.6g;
Carbs: 39.5g; Protein: 12.4g;
Sugars: 8.1g; Fiber: 6g

INGREDIENTS

- 3 ½ cups of cooked chickpeas (or 2 15-ounce cans of chickpeas, drained and rinsed)
- ½ cored and chopped, green bell pepper
- 1 finely chopped jalapeño (optional)
- 2 ½ cups of grape tomatoes (or cherry tomatoes), slice in halves if you like
- 3-5 green onions, cut into white and green portions
- ½ cup sun-dried tomatoes (use ones that have been preserved in jars with olive oil)
- 1/3 cup Kalamata olives, pitted
- ¼ cup green olives pitted
- ½ cup finely cut parsley leaves
- ½ cup finely chopped basil or mint leaves

For Dressing:
- ¼ cup Early Harvest Greek Extra virgin olive oil
- 2 tablespoons of white wine vinegar
- 2 tablespoons of lemon juice
- 1 minced garlic clove
- salt and black pepper
- 1 teaspoon of ground sumac
- ½ teaspoon of Aleppo pepper
- ¼ to ½ teaspoon of crushed red pepper (optional)

DIRECTIONS

1. Combine the chickpeas, veggies, sun-dried tomatoes, olives, and fresh herbs in a large bowl to make the salad.
2. Combine the extra virgin olive oil, white wine vinegar, lemon juice, minced garlic, salt, pepper, and spices to make the dressing in a separate, smaller bowl or jar.
3. Over the salad, drizzle the dressing and gently toss to combine. To serve, set aside for 30 minutes, or cover and chill in the refrigerator.
4. Give the salad a quick toss and taste before serving to check for any possible spice adjustments. Enjoy!

Arugula Salad with Pesto Shrimps, Parmesan and White Beans

PREP TIME: 25 min
COOK TIME: 10 min
TOTAL TIME: 35 min
SERVES: 2-4

NUTRITIONAL FACTS
Calories: 583; Fat: 43g; Carbs: 26g; Protein: 26g; Sugars: 7g; Fiber: 6g

INGREDIENTS

- ½ pound of Simple Truth raw jumbo shrimps, peeled and deveined
- 4 tablespoons of olive oil, divided
- 2 cloves garlic, pressed or minced
- ¼ teaspoon of kosher salt
- ¼ teaspoon of freshly ground black pepper
- pinch of red pepper flakes
- 2 cups of Private Selection cherry tomatoes
- ¼ cup of Hemispheres pesto
- 8 cups of Simple Truth baby arugula
- ½ lemon
- ⅛ cup of freshly shaved Parmesan cheese
- ½ cup of canned Simple Truth cannellini or other white beans, rinsed and drained.

DIRECTIONS

1. If the shrimps are frozen, defrost them in cool water, drain them, and then pat them dry before putting them in a bowl. Olive oil should be drizzled over the food before adding the garlic, kosher salt, pepper, and red pepper flakes. Allow the flavors to mingle for 20 to 30 minutes.
2. A nonstick skillet should be heated to medium-high. One tablespoon of the olive oil should be drizzled into the pan before adding the shrimps, which should be added one at a time and cooked in two batches. The shrimps should be cooked for 2 minutes on one side, flipped, and cooked just until opaque before being transferred to a bowl. The remainder of the shrimps, all the oil, garlic, and tomatoes from the bowl should be added to the skillet along with a modest reduction in heat. Cook for 4–5 minutes, tossing the tomatoes and garlic so that they don't burn and get bitter, and flipping the shrimps halfway through. Remove the skillet from the heat and add the remaining ingredients to the bowl with the shrimps.
3. Toss the arugula with your fingers in a bowl with the remaining olive oil and big squeeze of lemon juice. Sprinkle the tomatoes, beans, and all the garlicky pieces from the skillet over the arugula before adding the Parmesan. To taste, add additional kosher salt and freshly ground black pepper before tucking in.

Grilled Halloumi Salad Recipe

PREP TIME: 15 min
COOK TIME: 10 min
TOTAL TIME: 25 min
SERVES: 4

NUTRITIONAL FACTS
Calories: 510; Fat: 42g; Carbs: 13.8g; Protein: 19.2g; Sugars: 5g; Fiber: 2.7g

INGREDIENTS

- 75 g of a sourdough loaf
- 3 tablespoons of olive oil
- 1 tablespoon of finely shredded Parmesan or vegan hard cheese
- 250 g of thickly sliced halloumi
- 80 g of watercress, spinach, and rocket
- 100 g of lengthwise halved sugar snap peas
- 1 sliced avocado

Tomato-chili dressing:
- 3 tablespoons of olive oil
- 40 g chopped sun-dried tomatoes
- 1 tablespoon lemon juice
- ½ red chili, deseeded and finely chopped
- 200 g of cherry tomatoes (mixed colors if available), halved
- handful of fresh basil, finely chopped

DIRECTIONS

1. Preheat the oven to 380 F. Spread out the sourdough bread on a sizable baking sheet after roughly tearing it into bite-sized pieces. Sprinkle the grated Parmesan on top and drizzle with the remaining 2 tbsp of oil. Mix everything together until it is thoroughly covered. Bake for 7–8 minutes, or until crisp and golden.
2. In the meantime, combine all the dressing ingredients in a skillet over medium heat, excluding the cherry tomatoes and basil. After stirring for a minute, add the cherry tomatoes. Allow to soften in the dressing for two to three minutes, then turn off the heat and add the basil.
3. A sizable griddle pan should be hot. Add the halloumi slices to the pan in a single layer and drizzle with the remaining 1 tbsp oil. Cook until brown and charred, about 2 minutes per side.
4. In a sizable serving bowl, combine the avocado, sugar snap peas, and watercress salad. Add the halloumi and bread croutons on top. To serve, drizzle the warm tomato and chili dressing over the top.

Notes:
1. The croutons can be prepared ahead of time, completely cooled, and then kept for up to 24 hours in an airtight container.
2. Replace the Parmesan with a vegetarian hard cheese to make the salad vegetarian.

Spinach, Raspberry & Feta Salad

PREP TIME: 10 min
COOK TIME: 5 min
TOTAL TIME: 15 min
SERVES: 2

NUTRITIONAL FACTS
Calories: 220; Fat: 18g;
Carbs: 9g; Protein: 4g;
Sugars: 4g; Fiber: 3g

INGREDIENTS

- ¼ cup of olive oil
- 1 tablespoon of red wine vinegar
- 1 teaspoon of Dijon mustard
- ½ teaspoon of caster sugar
- 1 lemon
- 100 g of baby spinach leaves
- 120 g of fresh raspberries
- 1/3 cup of coarsely chopped pecans
- 100 g crumbled, drained Persian feta

DIRECTIONS

1. In a little screw-top jar, combine the mustard, sugar, oil, and vinegar. Add salt and pepper to taste. Shake vigorously to mix.
2. Zest the lemon using a zester. (Alternatively, peel the rind using a vegetable peeler. To remove the white pith and slice the rind into extremely thin strips, use a small, sharp knife.)
3. Add the spinach to a big bowl. Lemon rind, raspberries, pecans, and feta to be sprinkled on top.
4. On top of the salad, drizzle the dressing. Toss gently to blend.

Notes:
If you wish to make this recipe gluten-free, use gluten-free mustard. Picnic Tip: Add the dressing right before serving to keep the salad from becoming soggy. The dressing should be refrigerated immediately before leaving, along with the spinach combination, in an airtight container. Keep cold in a cooler.

Fresh Mango Guacamole

PREP TIME: 5 min
COOK TIME: 10 min
TOTAL TIME: 15 min
SERVES: 6

NUTRITIONAL FACTS
Calories: 254; Fat: 21g;
Carbs: 19g; Protein: 3g;
Sugars: 11g; Fiber: 3g

INGREDIENTS

- 3 big avocados
- 1 big mango
- 2 to 3 tablespoons of diced red onion, plus more for garnish
- 1 deseeded and minced jalapeño
- 1 lime, juiced
- 1/3 cup chopped cilantro, plus additional for garnish
- ½ teaspoon of cumin
- ½ teaspoon of coarse salt

DIRECTIONS

1. Cut the avocados in half, then remove the pits.
2. Slice the avocado long way through the peel and then across while it is on a cutting board. Gather the diced avocado and place it in a big bowl. Do this for each avocado.
3. With a fork, mash the avocado until it is split up but still chunky.
4. Hold the mango in your hand, thin side facing up. Slice the huge pit on either side. Cut into the flesh both longitudinally and across while holding the mango halves on a cutting board. Remove the mango and place it in the bowl with the avocado.
5. To the bowl, add the onion, jalapeños, lime juice, cilantro, cumin, and salt.
6. Mix well, then plate!

Salmon Caesar Salad

PREP TIME: 10 min
COOK TIME: 20 min
TOTAL TIME: 30 min
SERVES: 2

NUTRITIONAL FACTS
Calories: 594; Fat: 29g;
Carbs: 45g; Protein: 41g;
Sugars: 7g; Fiber: 5g

INGREDIENTS

- 8 ounces two fillets of pink salmon
- pinch of sea salt
- 1 tablespoon of olive oil

Croutons:
- ¼ of French loaf (~ 4oz)
- 1 tablespoon of olive oil
- 3 garlic cloves
- 1 teaspoon of sea salt

Salad:
- 1 romaine heart, coarsely chopped
- ¼ cup freshly grated Parmesan

Yogurt Caesar Dressing:
- 3 garlic cloves
- 4 anchovies
- 1 ½ lemons, juiced
- 1 tablespoon of yellow mustard
- 2 teaspoons of Worcestershire sauce
- ⅛ cup of Parmesan, freshly grated
- 1/3 cup of whole yogurt, plain

DIRECTIONS

1. Dry off the fish and set it aside. While you prepare the remainder of the salad, let the salmon come to room temperature.
2. Make Croutons. Set the oven to 350°F. Slice the bread into 1-inch squares. Garlic should be grated using a zester. (Alternatively, dice garlic thinly.)
3. Garlic, salt, and oil should be combined with the bread. Onto a baking sheet, spread. For soft croutons, bake for 11 minutes; for crunchy croutons, bake for 14 minutes.
4. Make dressing. Grate the garlic using a zester. (Alternatively, dice garlic thinly.) Add to the base of a sizable salad dish.
5. Anchovies can be added to the bowl. Use a pestle or a wooden spoon to mash the anchovies until they are completely broken down.
6. Add Worcestershire sauce, mustard, and lemon juice by whisking. Yogurt and Parmesan are added until smooth, whisk.
7. Pan-Sear the Salmon. Sprinkle salt over the salmon
8. A heavy bottom pan should be heated over medium-high heat with 1 TB of olive oil added. Add the salmon skin-side down when the oil is heated and starting to ripple, but DO NOT TOUCH THE SALMON.
9. Allow the salmon to sear for about two to three-quarters of the way through the fish, or until the translucent meat has cooked through and turned opaque. (As the fish cooks, you'll be able to observe how it becomes opaque from the bottom up.)
10. Reduce the heat a little if the fish in the pan starts to smoke. Use a thin metal spatula to flip the fish when it is halfway cooked through, and then sear the other side for 90 seconds. (Wait 30 seconds before attempting to flip the fish again if it refuses.)
11. Fish should be taken out of the pan and flaked using a fork. If desired, throw away the skin. To keep the fish warm, cover it.
12. Salad assembly. To the large bowl of dressing, add the diced romaine and the remaining Parmesan. The salad should be thoroughly mixed with the dressing until there is no longer any dressing remaining at the bottom of the bowl. Salmon and croutons should be added to the salad before serving.

CHAPTER 5
SOUP RECIPES

Greek Lentil Soup (Fakes)

PREP TIME: 10 min
COOK TIME: 1 h
TOTAL TIME: 1 h 10 min
SERVES: 4

NUTRITIONAL FACTS
Calories: 357; Fat: 16g;
Carbs: 40g; Protein: 16g;
Sugars: 4g; Fiber: 6g

INGREDIENTS

- 8 ounces brown lentils
- ¼ cup olive oil
- 1 medium onion, minced
- 1 big, diced carrot
- 1 tablespoon of garlic, minced
- 2 bay leaves
- 1 pinch of oregano, dried
- 1 pinch crushed dried rosemary
- 1 teaspoon of tomato pa ste
- black pepper and salt, to taste
- 1 teaspoon olive oil
- 1 teaspoon red wine vinegar

DIRECTIONS

1. To prepare the lentils, place them in a large pot and cover with water, making sure there is about an inch of water above the lentils. Bring the water to a boil and then let the lentils cook for 10 minutes. Drain the lentils after this time.

2. In a separate saucepan, heat up some olive oil over medium heat. Add the onion, carrot, and garlic and cook for about 5 minutes or until the onion becomes translucent. Once the vegetables have cooked, add the lentils to the saucepan along with a quart of water, bay leaves, oregano, and rosemary. Bring the mixture to a boil and then reduce the heat to medium-low. Let the lentils simmer for 10 minutes with the lid on.

3. After adding salt and pepper to taste, stir in some tomato paste. Cook the lentils, with the lid on, for 30 to 40 minutes, stirring occasionally. If the soup becomes too thick, add more water to thin it out. When you are ready to serve the lentils, drizzle them with red wine vinegar and olive oil.

Easy Thai Shrimp Soup

PREP TIME: 10 min
COOK TIME: 20 min
TOTAL TIME: 30 min
SERVES: 6

NUTRITIONAL FACTS
Calories: 368; Fat: 33g;
Carbs: 9g; Protein: 13g;
Sugars: 6g; Fiber: 5g

INGREDIENTS

- 1 cup of basmati rice, raw
- 2 teaspoons unsalted butter
- 1 pound medium shrimps, peeled and deveined
- freshly ground black pepper and kosher salt, to taste
- 2 minced garlic cloves
- 1 diced onion
- 1 chopped red bell pepper
- 1 tablespoon of ginger, freshly grated
- 2 tablespoons red curry paste
- 12 ounces of unsweetened coconut milk in a can
- 3 cups of vegetable stock
- 1 lime juice
- 2 tablespoons of freshly chopped cilantro leaves

DIRECTIONS

1. To prepare the rice, bring 1 ½ cups of water to a boil in a large saucepan. Add the rice and cook according to the package directions. Set the rice aside once it has finished cooking.

2. Melt some butter in a large stockpot or Dutch oven over medium-high heat. Add the shrimps, salt, and pepper to taste. Cook the shrimps for about 2–3 minutes, or until they turn pink. Once cooked, set the shrimps aside.

3. Add bell pepper, onion, and garlic to the stockpot. Stir the vegetables periodically and cook for 3–4 minutes, or until they are soft. For approximately a minute, stir in the ginger, until aromatic.

4. For approximately a minute, whisk in the curry paste until thoroughly incorporated. Add the coconut milk and vegetable stock gradually while whisking. Cook for 1–2 minutes, until thoroughly combined.

5. Bring to a boil; lower heat, and simmer for 8 to 10 minutes, or until just slightly thickened.

6. Add the cilantro, lime juice, and rice after stirring.

7. Serve right away.

Hearty Ground Turkey Soup with Vegetables

PREP TIME: 15 min
COOK TIME: 30 min
TOTAL TIME: 45 min
SERVES: 4

NUTRITIONAL FACTS
Calories: 408; Fat: 21g;
Carbs: 22g; Protein: 25g;
Sugars: 2g; Fiber: 3g

INGREDIENTS

- 1 lb of ground turkey
- 3 small Yukon gold potatoes
- 2 large carrots, peeled and chopped
- 1 medium zucchini squash, chopped
- 4 cups chicken stock
- 4 slices thick-cut bacon, chopped
- ½ yellow onion, diced
- full-fat coconut milk one (15-ounce) can
- 3 cups of young spinach
- ½ teaspoon of sea salt

DIRECTIONS

1. First, heat a Dutch oven or large pot. Once heated, add the chopped bacon and cook for 2–3 minutes until most of the fat has been rendered.
2. Next, add the onion and stir periodically for approximately 5 minutes until the onion becomes transparent.
3. Add the ground turkey after pushing the onions to the side of the pot (or sausage). After flipping, continue browning for an additional one to two minutes. Cut the meat into smaller pieces using a spatula.
4. Except for the spinach, add the remaining ingredients to the pot, cover it, and bring to a full boil. The potatoes should be cooked all the way through after 20 to 30 minutes at a medium boil. For an additional 2 to 3 minutes, add the spinach after stirring.

Slow Cooker Split Pea Soup

PREP TIME: 10 min
COOK TIME: 5 h
TOTAL TIME: 5 h 10 min
SERVES: 6

NUTRITIONAL FACTS
Calories: 299; Fat: 8g;
Carbs: 55g; Protein: 20g;
Sugars: 10g; Fiber: 22g

INGREDIENTS

- 1 pound of split peas, rinsed and picked over
- 1 medium yellow onion, diced
- 1 cup of celery, diced
- 2 cups of carrot, diced
- 3 cloves of garlic, minced or finely grated
- 1 to 2 bay leaves
- 1 teaspoon smoked paprika
- ½ tablespoon kosher salt
- 1 quart of chicken stock or veggie broth
- 2-cups of water

Optional
- 1 ham hock and two cups of chopped ham

To add at the end:
- 1 tablespoon of red wine vinegar or fresh lemon juice for flavor

DIRECTIONS

1. In a 6-quart slow cooker, add the split peas, onion, celery, carrot, garlic, bay leaves, smoked paprika, salt, broth, water, and ham or ham bone (if using). Stir to incorporate.
2. Cover and cook for 5–6 hours on high or 7–8 hours on low. Don't open the lid while the food is cooking.
3. Uncover, add the red wine vinegar, and blend. If using, take the ham bone out and throw it away. If necessary, taste and add more vinegar or salt. Top with your preferred toppings before serving

Stove Top Instructions:

1. In a sizable saucepan or Dutch oven, combine the split peas, onion, celery, carrot, garlic, bay leaves, smoked paprika, salt, broth, water, and the ham or ham bone (if using). Stir to incorporate.
2. Cover, heat to a boil, then lower the heat, so it simmers. Cook on low for 40–50 minutes, or until the soup has thickened, and the peas are thoroughly cooked.
3. Take off the top, add the red wine vinegar, and blend. If using, take the ham bone out and throw it away. If necessary, taste and add more vinegar or salt. Top with your preferred toppings before serving

Notes:

Allowing this soup to chill for around 30 minutes before serving will give it a somewhat thicker consistency, since it thickens quite a little as it cools.

Veggistrone

PREP TIME: 15 min
COOK TIME: 1 h 30 min
TOTAL TIME: 1 h 45 min
SERVES: 10

NUTRITIONAL FACTS
Calories: 162; Fat: 4.7g;
Carbs: 24.4g; Protein: 7.2g;
Sugars: 9g; Fiber: 8.6g

INGREDIENTS

- 2 tablespoons olive oil, Extra virgin
- 2 cups of onions, chopped (2 medium)
- 2 cups of celery, chopped (4 medium stalks)
- 1 cup finely chopped green pepper (1 medium)
- 4 minced garlic cloves
- 3 cups of chopped kale
- 3 cups chopped (about medium-sized) cauliflower
- 2 cups of carrots, chopped (4 medium)
- 2 cups green beans, frozen, thawed, and chopped into 1-inch pieces
- 8 cups of low-sodium chicken or veggie broth
- 2 cups of water
- 15 ounces of tomato sauce in one can
- 1 can of diced tomatoes (14 ounces)
- 1 (15 ounce) can of washed pinto or kidney beans
- bay leaf, one
- 1 box of 10 ounces of frozen chopped spinach, thawed, or 4 cups of fresh spinach, chopped
- ½ cup of thinly sliced basil
- 10 teaspoons freshly grated Parmesan cheese

DIRECTIONS

1. Over medium heat, warm the oil in a big soup pot or Dutch oven (8 quarts or bigger). Add the bell pepper, onions, celery, and garlic; simmer for 13 to 15 minutes, stirring frequently, until softened. Cook, stirring periodically, then added cabbage, cauliflower, carrots, and green beans for a further 10 minutes or until slightly softened.
2. Add the beans, bay leaf, tomato sauce, broth, water, and tomatoes. Put the pot's lid on and then bring it to a boil. Reduce heat and cook the vegetables for 20 to 25 minutes with a half-cover. Add spinach and cook for an additional 10 minutes.
3. Throw away the bay leaf. Stir in basil. One tablespoon of cheese is added to each serving.

> Notes:
> To make this recipe in advance, you can prepare everything up to Step 2 and store it in the refrigerator for up to 5 days, or in the freezer for up to 6 months. When you're ready to serve, complete Step 3 just before serving.

Roasted Cauliflower & Potato Curry Soup

PREP TIME: 20 min
COOK TIME: 1 h 10 min
TOTAL TIME: 1 h 30 min
SERVES: 8

NUTRITIONAL FACTS
Calories: 272; Fat: 14.8g;
Carbs: 33.4g; Protein: 5.3g;
Sugars: 8.3g; Fiber: 7.2g

INGREDIENTS

- 2 teaspoons of ground coriander
- 2 teaspoons of ground cumin
- 1 ½ teaspoons of ground cinnamon
- 1 ½ teaspoons of ground turmeric
- 1 ¼ teaspoons of salt
- ¾ teaspoon of ground pepper
- ⅛ teaspoon of cayenne pepper
- 1 small cauliflower head, divided into tiny florets (about 6 cups)
- 2 tablespoons of Extra virgin olive oil
- 1 big, chopped onion
- 3 huge cloves of minced garlic and one cup of diced carrot
- 1 ½ tablespoons freshly grated ginger
- 1 minced fresh red chili pepper, such as a jalapeño or serrano, plus more ones for garnish
- 1 (14 ounce) can of tomato sauce with no salt added
- 4 cups of vegetable broth low in salt
- 3 cups chopped, peeled, and thick-cut russet potatoes
- 3 cups of chopped, peeled, and thickly cut sweet potatoes
- 2 tablespoons lime juice and 2 teaspoons lime zest
- 14 ounces coconut milk can
- fresh cilantro chopped for garnish

DIRECTIONS

1. Set the oven to 450°F.
2. Mix together in a small bowl the coriander, cumin, cinnamon, turmeric, salt, pepper, and cayenne. In a big bowl, combine the cauliflower with 1 tablespoon of oil. Then, add 1 tablespoon of the spice combination, and toss once more. On a baking sheet with a rim, spread out in a single layer. 15 to 20 minutes of roasting the cauliflower is sufficient to brown the edges. Place aside.
3. In the meantime, in a big pot over medium-high heat, warm the last tablespoon of oil. Cook the onion and carrot for 3 to 4 minutes, turning frequently, until they begin to color. Reduce heat to medium and sauté the onion for 3 to 4 minutes, stirring often. Add the remaining spice blend, along with the garlic, ginger, and chili. Cook for another minute while stirring.
4. After scraping off any browned parts, add the tomato sauce and boil for one minute. Add the broth, sweet potatoes, potatoes, lime juice, and zest. Over high heat, cover and bring to a boil. Cook, partially covered, and stirring periodically, for 35 to 40 minutes, or until the veggies are soft. Reduce the temperature to keep a gentle simmering.
5. Add coconut milk and the roasted cauliflower after stirring. Bring back to a simmer to finish heating. If preferred, serve with cilantro and chilies as garnish.

Red Lentil Soup with Saffron

PREP TIME: 20 min
COOK TIME: 20 min
TOTAL TIME: 40 min
SERVES: 8

NUTRITIONAL FACTS
Calories: 280; Fat: 7g;
Carbs: 42g; Protein: 15g;
Sugars: 3g; Fiber: 8g

INGREDIENTS

- 3 teaspoons Extra virgin olive oil
- 2 medium carrots, diced finely
- 2 celery stalks, diced finely
- 1 large onion, chopped
- 3 minced garlic cloves
- 1 teaspoon of tomato paste
- ½ teaspoon of cumin seeds
- ¼ teaspoon crushed saffron threads
- ¼ teaspoon of powdered turmeric
- 4 cups low-sodium chicken broth or no-chicken broth
- 1 ½ cups water, and additional liquid as needed
- 1 pound (2 cups) of rinsed and inspected red lentils
- 5 ounces of finely chopped spinach
- 1 teaspoon kosher salt
- 1 teaspoon of pepper, ground
- plain yogurt with freshly chopped mint as a garnish

DIRECTIONS

1. Over medium heat, warm the oil in a big, heavy pot. Cook the carrots, celery, and onion for 7 to 10 minutes, or until they begin to soften (never brown). Cook for one minute after stirring in the garlic, tomato paste, cumin, saffron, and turmeric.
2. Salt, pepper, lentils, water, and broth should all be added. Simmer for a while. In order to prevent sticking, adjust the heat to a simmer, cover the pot, and cook the lentils and veggies for 15 to 20 minutes, stirring occasionally. Should you wish, add more water.
3. If desired, garnish with yogurt and mint.

Mediterranean-Style Fish Soup Recipe

PREP TIME: 10 min
COOK TIME: 25 min
TOTAL TIME: 35 min
SERVES: 5

NUTRITIONAL FACTS
Calories: 207; Fat: 2.1g;
Carbs: 16.6g; Protein: 28g;
Sugars: 3g; Fiber: 4.2g

INGREDIENTS

- 1 ½ teaspoons of coriander
- 1 teaspoon of cumin
- 1 teaspoon of red pepper flakes or Aleppo pepper flakes
- ¾ teaspoon of turmeric
- ½ teaspoon of paprika
- mixture of sea bass and red snapper, weighing 1 ½ pounds, chopped it into chunks (1 1/2 inch pieces)
- salt with black pepper kosher
- 3 teaspoons Extra virgin olive oil
- 1 chopped red onion
- 1 chopped red bell pepper
- 2 ribs of celery, diced
- 4 minced garlic cloves
- 1 can (28-ounce) of whole tomatoes
- ½ cup of white wine
- 4 cups of low-sodium chicken or vegetable stock, preferred
- 1 cup of fresh parsley, chopped and packaged
- 1 cup of fresh cilantro, chopped and packed
- 3 chopped green onions, including the white and green parts
- lemon juice

DIRECTIONS

1. Gather the spices and combine them in a small bowl.
2. Add 2 to 3 tablespoons of the spice combination to the fish, along with a generous pinch of kosher salt and black pepper, and toss to coat.
3. Three tablespoons of extra virgin olive oil are heated over medium-high heat in a big saucepan or Dutch oven. Put in the celery, onions, bell peppers, and garlic. Cook for 5 minutes, stirring frequently, or until the vegetables soften. Add a generous amount of black pepper and kosher salt for seasoning. The remaining spice mixture should be added.
4. Tomatoes, white wine, and chicken broth should be added. After coming to a boil, reduce the heat to medium-low. Let the pot simmer for 20 minutes with a partial cover on.
5. Cook the fish for 4 to 5 minutes, or until it is well cooked, after adding it (do not over-cook the fish, remember it will continue to cook in the hot broth even after you remove it from the heat).
6. Add the parsley, cilantro, and green onions and stir. Add lemon juice to finish. Serve right away.

Notes:

1. Which fish fillet should I use? Here, a fish fillet with a relatively firm texture works well. I combined red snapper and sea bass, as specified in the recipe. Cod and halibut are also excellent choices.
2. Leftovers. Depending on how fresh the fish was when you cooked it, fish soup can be kept in the refrigerator for 2 to 3 days. I prefer to remove the fish to thoroughly warm the broth before adding it back in, which prevents the fish from overcooking.

Sweet Potato Black Bean Soup

PREP TIME: 20 min
COOK TIME: 20 min
TOTAL TIME: 40 min
SERVES: 6

NUTRITIONAL FACTS
Calories: 174; Fat: 1g;
Carbs: 39g; Protein: 6g;
Sugars: 2g; Fiber: 6g

INGREDIENTS

- 32 ounces of vegetable broth
- 4 cups sweet potatoes, diced and peeled
- 1 (15 ounce) can of rinsed and drained black beans with reduced sodium
- 1 cup mild picante sauce
- 12 ounces coarsely chopped roasted red peppers
- ¼ cup chopped cilantro
- 1 tablespoon smoked paprika
- 2 medium limes, juice

DIRECTIONS

1. Over medium-high heat, combine sweet potatoes and vegetable broth. Cook for 7 minutes after bringing to a boil to soften the sweet potatoes.
2. Black beans and picante sauce should be blended together in the meantime until smooth.
3. To the soup, incorporate the black bean combination and roasted red peppers. Warm up less. Add lime juice, cilantro, and smoked paprika. Cook soup with a stir for 5 to 7 minutes, or until well heated.

Mediterranean white Bean Soup

PREP TIME: 10 min
COOK TIME: 25 min
TOTAL TIME: 35 min
SERVES: 6

NUTRITIONAL FACTS
Calories: 295; Fat: 3g;
Carbs: 52g; Protein: 17g;
Sugars: 3g; Fiber: 12g

INGREDIENTS

- 1 large onion, diced
- 1 tablespoon of olive oil
- 2 minced garlic cloves
- 2-3 sliced big carrots
- 2-3 sliced celery stalks
- 6 cups of vegetable stock
- ½ teaspoon oregano
- 1 teaspoon salt
- ½ teaspoon black pepper
- 1 teaspoon dried thyme
- 3 cans of 15-ounce white beans, washed and drain,
- 2 cups baby spinach
- finely chopped fresh parsley for serving
- for serving, grated Parmesan cheese

DIRECTIONS

1. Heat olive oil over medium-high heat in a big pot or saucepan. Add the onions and simmer for 3 to 5 minutes until they are transparent. Cook for an additional two to three minutes before incorporating the garlic, carrots, celery, thyme, oregano, salt, and pepper.
2. To mix all the flavors, add beans and vegetable broth, bring to a boil, then lower the heat and cook for 15 minutes.
3. Add the spinach and simmer for 2 minutes, or until the spinach wilts.
4. Fresh parsley and grated Parmesan cheese may be added after the dish has been taken off the heat.

CHAPTER 6
DESSERT RECIPES

Avocado Chocolate Mousse

PREP TIME: 5 min
COOK TIME: 15 min
TOTAL TIME: 20 min
SERVES: 4

NUTRITIONAL FACTS
Calories: 596; Fat: 42g;
Carbs: 92g; Protein: 26g;
Sugars: 12g; Fiber: 4g

INGREDIENTS

- 1 ¼ cups of canned coconut milk or unsweetened almond milk
- 1 pound of finely chopped, dairy-free dark chocolate, preferably 60% cacao
- 4 small ripe avocado pitted, peeled, and diced
- ¼ cup agave syrup
- 2 tablespoons of puffy quinoa
- 1 tablespoon of finely grated orange zest
- 2 tablespoons of sea salt from Maldon
- 2 tablespoons of flakes of Aleppo pepper
- 1 tablespoon of Extra virgin olive oil

DIRECTIONS

1. Heat the almond or coconut milk in a small saucepan over medium-high heat until an instant-read thermometer reads 175°F. Chop the chocolate, remove from the fire, and mix until smooth. Allow to cool to room temperature.
2. Place the avocados, agave, orange zest, and chilled chocolate mixture in a blender and blend on high until smooth.
3. Distribute the mousse among four bowls for serving. Puffed quinoa, sea salt, Aleppo pepper, and olive oil should all be uniformly distributed.

Peaches-and-Cream Ice Pops

PREP TIME: 10 min
COOK TIME: 40 min
ADDITIONAL TIME: 2 h
TOTAL TIME: 2 h 50 min
SERVES: 8

NUTRITIONAL FACTS
Calories: 121; Fat: 5g;
Carbs:18g; Protein: 4g;
Sugars: 15g; Fiber: 3g

INGREDIENTS

- 1 pound (450 g) of peaches, wedged and peeled
- 65g or 1/3 cup of light brown sugar
- ½ teaspoon of cinnamon powder
- pinch of sea salt, fine
- 1½ cups (340g) of unflavored Greek yogurt
- ½ cup (110 grams) of crème fraîche
- 2 teaspoons of pure vanilla extract
- ¼ teaspoon of pure almond extract

DIRECTIONS

1. Set the oven to 375 °F. Place the peaches on a baking sheet in an equal layer. Salt, cinnamon, and brown sugar are added; blend by tossing.
2. Roast the peaches for 20 to 25 minutes, or until fork-tender. 15 minutes to cool.
3. Combine the yogurt, crème fraîche, vanilla, and almond extract in a big bowl. About three-quarters of the mixture should be transferred to a container with a pour spout.
4. Combine the remaining yogurt mixture in the basin with the chilled peaches. Combine the two using a potato masher; it's fine if there are still peach bits.
5. Fill each ice-pop mold with 2 teaspoons of the yogurt mixture. 4 tablespoons of the peach mixture should be added next, and then 4 tablespoons of the yogurt mixture. Till the molds are full, alternate the two as before. The layers blending together is acceptable.
6. Insert an ice-pop stick in the middle of each mold before freezing. Freeze for at least two hours, until solid.
7. Warm up the molds in water before removing the ice pops. Till you are ready to serve, keep frozen.

Rosé Poached Pears with Ginger and Vanilla

PREP TIME: 10 min
COOK TIME: 25 min
TOTAL TIME: 35 min
SERVES: 6

NUTRITIONAL FACTS
Calories: 277; Fat: 0g;
Carbs: 49g; Protein: 1g;
Sugars: 35g; Fiber: 4g

INGREDIENTS

- 1 bottle of dry rosé wine
- ½ cup of sugar
- 1 inch of peeled fresh ginger
- 1 vanilla bean, lengthwise split
- 6 peeled pears
- whipped cream

DIRECTIONS

1. Simmer the rosé wine, sugar, and ginger in a big pot. Add the vanilla seeds after scraping the pod out. Stir the sugar until it melts.
2. Gently lower the pears into the liquid, making sure they are completely submerged if additional water is required.
3. Simmer for 20 to 25 minutes, or until the pears are quite soft. Pears should be taken out of the liquid and totally cooled.
4. Boil the liquid until it is reduced to about 3/4 cup of syrupy liquid
5. Arrange each pear on a tiny platter before serving. Each pear should receive 2 tablespoons of syrup, and whipped cream should be served right away.

No-Bake, Gluten-Free Rose Petal Brownie

PREP TIME: 10 min
COOK TIME: 25 min
ADDITIONAL TIME: 2 h
TOTAL TIME: 2 h 35 min
SERVES: 8

NUTRITIONAL FACTS
Calories: 531; Fat: 27g;
Carbs: 75g; Protein: 9g;
Sugars: 59g; Fiber: 2g

INGREDIENTS

Base
- cooking spray, for pan
- 2 1/3 cups of pitted dates
- 1 1/3 cups of almonds
- 1/3 cup of cocoa powder
- 2 teaspoons of pure vanilla extract
- ¼ teaspoon of fine sea salt
- 1 cup dried of cherries
- 1 cup roughly chopped macadamia nuts

Topping
- ¼ cup of cocoa powder
- ¼ cup of maple syrup
- 2 tablespoons of melted coconut oil
- fresh or dried rose petals, for finishing

DIRECTIONS

1. Make the base: Apply cooking spray to an 8-inch square baking pan, then line it with parchment paper.
2. Process the dates, almonds, cocoa powder, salt, vanilla essence, and 1 tablespoon of water in a food processor bowl until the mixture is extremely smooth. Place the mixture in the pan and spread it out evenly.
3. Distribute and lightly press the macadamia nuts and cherries into the base.
4. Make the topping: Combine the cocoa powder, maple syrup, and coconut oil in a medium bowl. Pour onto the base, then level out into a layer. Add rose petals as a garnish.
5. Put the pan in the fridge and let it cold for at least two hours. Serve right away, or keep in the fridge for up to a week.

Baked Blueberry & Banana-Nut Oatmeal Cups

PREP TIME: 15 min
COOK TIME: 35 min
TOTAL TIME: 50 min
SERVES: 12

NUTRITIONAL FACTS
Calories: 181; Fat: 6g; Carbs: 28g; Protein: 5g; Sugars: 12g; Fiber: 3g

INGREDIENTS

- 3 cups of oats
- 1½ cups of nonfat milk
- 2 ripe bananas, mashed (about 3/4 cup)
- 1/3 cup of brown sugar
- 2 big, lightly beaten eggs
- 1 teaspoon of baking powder
- 1 teaspoon of ground cinnamon
- 1 teaspoon of vanilla extract
- ½ teaspoon of salt
- 1 cup of fresh blueberries
- ½ cup of chopped toasted pecans

DIRECTIONS

1. Preheat the oven to 375°F. Spray cooking oil into a muffin pan.
2. Mix the following ingredients in a sizable bowl: oats, milk, bananas, brown sugar, eggs, baking powder, cinnamon, vanilla, and salt. Mix in the pecans and blueberries. Place a small amount of the mixture (approximately 1/3 cup) in each muffin cup. Bake for about 25 minutes, or until a toothpick inserted in the center comes out clean. After cooling in the pan for ten minutes, remove and place on a wire rack. At room temperature or heated, serve.

Baked Pears with Maple Syrup and Almond Crumble

PREP TIME: 15 min
COOK TIME: 15 min
TOTAL TIME: 30 min
SERVES: 6

NUTRITIONAL FACTS
Calories: 292; Fat: 12g; Carbs: 47g; Protein: 2g; Sugars: 32g; Fiber: 0g

INGREDIENTS

Baked Pears
- 4 pears, cut in half
- 2 tablespoons of unsalted butter
- ½ cup of maple syrup
- 1 teaspoon of pure vanilla extract
- ¼ teaspoon of ground cinnamon

Almond Crumble
- 2 tablespoons of unsalted butter
- ½ cup of rolled oats
- ¼ cup of sliced almonds
- 2 tablespoons of pure maple syrup
- 1 tablespoon of heavy cream
- ½ teaspoon of ground cinnamon
- ¼ teaspoon of fine sea salt
- whipped cream, for serving

DIRECTIONS

Make the Baked Pears:
1. Set the oven to 400°F. Use a spoon or melon baller to remove the seeds from the center of each pear half. Then, place the pear halves on a baking sheet lined with parchment paper.
2. Melt the butter in a small pot over medium heat. Add cinnamon, vanilla essence, and maple syrup after stirring.
3. Liberally brush the pears with the maple syrup mixture all over. The sliced sides of the pears should now be pointing downward.
4. Bake the pears for 15 to 20 minutes, or until they are soft.

Make the Almond Crumble:
1. Melt the butter in a small pot over medium heat while the pears bake. Stir the oats and almonds for about 3 minutes, until they begin to smell slightly toasted. Heavy cream and maple syrup are then added, and the mixture is cooked for about 3 minutes, or until it slightly thickens. Add salt and cinnamon and stir. Place in a bowl and allow cooling.
2. Top the warm pears with whipped cream and crumbled pie crust.

Easy Lemon Bars - Delicious & Dairy Free

COOK TIME: 30 min
TOTPREP TIME: 10 min
AL TIME: 40 min
SERVES: 15

NUTRITIONAL FACTS
Calories: 130; Fat: 5.8g;
Carbs: 1.5g; Protein: 1.7g;
Sugars: 12g; Fiber: 2g

INGREDIENTS

- 1 cup coconut oil/or vegan butter (softened)
- 1/3 cup of coconut sugar
- 2 cups of all-purpose flour
- 1¼ cup of white sugar (separated from other sugar)
- 4 big eggs
- 1/4 teaspoon of lemon zest
- 2 lemons, seeded, juiced, yielding at least ½ cup or more
- ¼ cup of all-purpose flour

DIRECTIONS

1. Blend the flour, 1/3 cup coconut sugar, and softened coconut or vegan butter in a bowl. This will serve as the lemon bars' crust. Place the mixture in a greased 9x13 pan, and then use your fingers to push down firmly to create the crust.
2. 16 to 18 minutes on 350 degrees for the crust (or until it's a golden color)
3. Mix ¼ cup of flour and the remaining sugar in a bowl. The eggs, lemon zest, and juice are whisked together, then slowly added to the dry ingredients. Pour this mixture over the crust once it has baked.
4. Put back in the oven for a further 15 to 18 minutes of baking. Try not to overcook them because they will firm up more once they cool.

Cocoa & Cherry Oat Bake

PREP TIME: 15 min
COOK TIME: 30 min
TOTAL TIME: 45 min
SERVES: 6

NUTRITIONAL FACTS
Calories: 289; Fat: 13g;
Carbs: 30g; Protein: 9g;
Sugars: 8g; Fiber: 7g

INGREDIENTS

- 75 g of dried cherries
- 1 tablespoon of chia seeds
- 500 ml of hazelnut milk
- 200 g of jumbo oats
- 3 tablespoons of cocoa powder
- 1 tablespoon of cocoa nibs
- 1 teaspoon of baking powder
- 1 teaspoon of vanilla extract
- 50 g of blanched hazelnuts
- fat-free yogurt and sugar-free cherry compote, to serve (optional)

DIRECTIONS

1. Turn on the oven's gas 6, 380°F. Boiling water should cover the cherries; leave for 10 minutes. In the meantime, combine 3 tbsp warm water with the chia seeds.
2. Drain the cherries and combine them with the soaked chia seeds and other remaining ingredients (apart from the hazelnuts), in a large bowl. Pour the mixture into a 2-liter ovenproof dish, top with the hazelnuts, and bake for 25 to 30 minutes, or until the center is scalding hot. If desired, top with cherry compote and yogurt.

Greek Orange Honey Cake with Pistachios

PREP TIME: 10 min
COOK TIME: 30 min
TOTAL TIME: 40 min
SERVES: 12

NUTRITIONAL FACTS
Calories: 379; Fat: 10g;
Carbs: 57g; Protein: 8g;
Sugars: 44g; Fiber: 5g

INGREDIENTS

For Cake
- 5 big eggs
- 1 cup of Greek yogurt with low-fat
- 2 cups of sugar, granulated
- 5 tablespoons of ground almonds
- 1 Meyer lemon zest
- 1 orange zest
- 1 ¼ cup of all-purpose flour
- 1 cup of coarse semolina (or farina, Cream of Wheat, or this Creamy Wheat Cereal)
- 2 teaspoons of baking powder
- ¾ cup plus 1 tablespoon Private Reserve Greek Extra virgin olive oil
- Handful of shaved almonds for topping, optional

For Honey Pistachio Syrup
- 1 ¼ cup shelled salted pistachios
- 1 ¼ cup of runny honey
- 2 oranges (juice)
- 1 lemon (juice)

DIRECTIONS

1. Set the oven to 350 °F.
2. To prepare a 9 x 13 baking pan for a cake, first grease it with butter and coat it evenly with flour by shaking the pan.
3. Next, in a large mixing bowl, combine all ingredients for the cake batter (excluding shaved almonds) and mix until well blended, using a wooden spoon or whisk.
4. Spread the mixture evenly with a spatula after pouring it into the prepared baking pan.
5. Bake for 25 to 30 minutes in a hot oven, or until golden and well done. To test whether the cake is done, stick a wooden skewer into the center; it should come out clean.
6. Take the cake out of the oven and allow it to cool completely in the pan.
7. Prepare the honey syrup after the cake has cooled. In a dry nonstick pan over low to medium heat, toast the pistachios. Add the honey and stir once they begin to smell. Lemon and orange juices should be added. For 1 to 2 minutes, or until nice and syrupy, bring to a boil.
8. Use a small knife or a skewer to make holes all over the cake. As evenly as you can, drizzle the honey-pistachio syrup over the entire cake. If necessary, spread the pistachios evenly over the cake's top with a spoon. Add some almond shavings, if desired.
9. At this stage, you can cut the cake into 12 to 15 squares and serve.

Notes: For the cake to absorb the syrup more effectively, the syrup must be hot when you pour it over the cooled cake. Additionally, let the cake sit for a few hours before cutting and serving for optimal results.

CHAPTER 7
SMOOTHIE RECIPES

Post-Workout Green Smoothie

PREP TIME: 10 min
COOK TIME: 1 min
TOTAL TIME: 11 min
SERVES: 2

NUTRITIONAL FACTS
Calories: 226; Fat: 7g;
Carbs: 34g; Protein: 9g;
Sugars: 16g; Fiber: 10g

INGREDIENTS

- 2 cups of filtered water
- 2 cups of baby spinach
- 1 frozen, sliced banana
- 1 green apple
- ¼ avocado
- 2 tablespoons of collagen powder
- 2 tablespoons of protein powder
- 2 tablespoons of chia seeds

DIRECTIONS

Put all the ingredients in a blender. Blend until smooth after 30 seconds.

Anti-Inflammatory Cherry-Spinach Smoothie

PREP TIME: 5 min
COOK TIME: 2 min
TOTAL TIME: 7 min
SERVES: 1-2

NUTRITIONAL FACTS
Calories: 410; Fat: 20g;
Carbs: 46g; Protein: 17g;
Sugars: 33g; Fiber: 10g

INGREDIENTS

- 1 cup of unflavored low-fat kefir
- 1 cup frozen cherries
- ½ cup of young spinach leaves
- ¼ cup mashed ripe avocado
- salted almond butter in one spoonful
- peeled ginger cut into 1 (½ inch) pieces
- 1 tablespoon of chia seeds plus extra for decoration

DIRECTIONS

Place kefir in a blender. Blend till smooth the cherries, spinach, avocado, almond butter, ginger, and chia seeds. Pour into a glass; if desired, top with extra chia seeds.

Jamu Juice - Turmeric Ginger Drink

PREP TIME: 5 min
COOK TIME: 20 min
TOTAL TIME: 25 min
SERVES: 8

NUTRITIONAL FACTS
Calories: 97; Fat: 2g;
Carbs: 20g; Protein: 2g;
Sugars: 8g; Fiber: 5g

INGREDIENTS

- 125 g of fresh turmeric, finely chopped into 1 cup
- 20 g of fresh ginger
- 4 cups coconut water
- 2 tablespoons of honey or another sweetener
- 1 lemon, juice
- black pepper (optional)

DIRECTIONS

1. Slice thin disks of ginger and turmeric. You are welcome to keep the skin on.
2. To a blender, add the coconut water, ginger, black pepper, and turmeric. Until the mixture is smooth, blend on high for about a minute.
3. The mixture should boil after being poured into a pot. Turn the heat down to low and simmer the mixture for 20 minutes. After that, whisk everything well before adding the honey and lemon juice.
4. Use a fine mesh sieve, nut milk bag, or muslin towel to strain the mixture. Pour the mixture into a glass container and put it in the fridge. Enjoy warm or cold.

Notes:
I believe that fresh turmeric works best in this dish, you can also use turmeric powder. Typically, 1 cup of fresh turmeric is equal to 1/3 cup of turmeric powder.

Anti-Inflammatory Smoothie

PREP TIME: 5 min
COOK TIME: 2 min
TOTAL TIME: 7 min
SERVES: 1-2

NUTRITIONAL FACTS
Calories: 119; Fat: 3g; Carbs: 24g; Protein: 3g; Sugars: 15g; Fiber: 4g

INGREDIENTS

- 1 cup kale
- ½ beet peeled and chopped
- ½ cup of water
- ½ orange peeled
- 1 cup mixed berries (frozen)
- ½ cup of frozen pineapple
- 1 teaspoon of ginger root grated or chopped
- 1 teaspoon of coconut oil
- 1 serving Protein Smoothie Boost (optional)

DIRECTIONS

1. Combine baby kale, beet, water, and orange in a blender.
2. Blend until everything is evenly combined.
3. Add the rest of the ingredients and blend until well combined and fluid.

Notes:
Beets can be replaced by carrots.
Mango can be used in place of pineapple.
To make the smoothie less bitter, add baby kale or spinach.

Blueberry Protein Shake | Thick & Refreshing

PREP TIME: 5 min
COOK TIME: 5 min
TOTAL TIME: 10 min
SERVES: 1-2

NUTRITIONAL FACTS
Calories: 193; Fat: 12 g; Carbs: 32g; Protein: 31g; Sugars: 22g; Fiber: 3g

INGREDIENTS

- ¾ cup of unsweetened almond milk or milk of choice
- ½ cup of full-fat Greek yogurt
- 1 scoop vanilla protein powder
- ¾ cup of frozen blueberries
- 3–4 ice cubes, if a thicker texture is desired
- 1 teaspoon of raw honey optional for added sweetness

DIRECTIONS

1. To start, place all ingredients into a blender, beginning with the almond milk. Using your blender's appropriate settings, begin by blending the ice and frozen blueberries to create a smooth texture. If you prefer, you can omit the ice at the beginning and gradually add it in as you blend the rest of the ingredients.
2. Continuously blend and add ice until you reach your desired consistency. If the mixture becomes too thick, gradually add additional almond milk. If it's not sweet enough, add a little extra honey to taste.

Kiwi and Kale Smoothie

PREP TIME: 2 min
COOK TIME: 2 min
TOTAL TIME: 4 min
SERVES: 1-2

NUTRITIONAL FACTS
Calories: 166; Fat: 5.7g; Carbs: 39g; Protein: 6.4g; Sugars: 16.9g; Fiber: 10g

INGREDIENTS

- 1 ripe banana
- 1 sliced and peeled ripe kiwi
- ½ cup of kale, cleaned and neatly packed
- 1 cup of almond milk without sugar
- 1 teaspoon optional raw honey
- 1 tablespoon flaxseed meal
- ½ cup of ice

DIRECTIONS

1. Place the ice, banana, kale, kiwi, raw honey, flaxseed meal, and unsweetened almond milk in a blender.
2. Combine all the ingredients and blend until a smooth consistency is achieved. Depending on the strength of your blender, you may need to blend the kale for at least a minute to fully purée it.
3. If the drink is too thick, add a little more almond milk to thin it out. If it's too thin, add more ice and blend again to thicken it up.

Notes:
Add 1 scoop of vanilla or unflavored protein powder to this smoothie to boost the protein content and turn it into a complete meal.

Pineapple-Grapefruit Detox Smoothie

PREP TIME: 2 min
COOK TIME: 2 min
TOTAL TIME: 4 min
SERVES: 1-2

NUTRITIONAL FACTS
Calories: 102; Fat: 0.2g;
Carbs: 25g; Protein: 2g;
Sugars: 19g; Fiber: 2.9g

INGREDIENTS

- 1 cup of plain coconut water
- 1 cup of frozen pineapple dice
- 1 cup of baby spinach
- 1 small grapefruit, peeled and cut into segments, including any membrane juice
- ½ teaspoon of freshly grated ginger
- 1 cup of ice

DIRECTIONS

In a blender, combine ice, ginger, coconut water, pineapple, spinach, grapefruit, and any liquids. Blend until frothy and smooth.

Creamy Pineapple Cucumber Smoothie

PREP TIME: 3 min
COOK TIME: 2 min
TOTAL TIME: 4 min
SERVES: 1

NUTRITIONAL FACTS
Calories: 225; Fat: 3.9g;
Carbs: 52g; Protein: 6g;
Sugars: 28g; Fiber: 7.9g

INGREDIENTS

- ½ cup of cucumber slices, preferably organic and with the peel on
- 1 large cup of diced pineapple (if frozen, omit ice)
- ½ large ripe, peeled, frozen banana
- ¼ cup light coconut milk
- ½ cup of filtered water
- 2 tablespoons (30 ml) of juice and 1 teaspoon of zest from 1 medium lime
- 1 huge handful of greens, preferably organic (spinach or kale)
- 2–4 cubes of ice

DIRECTIONS

1. Blend the following ingredients in a blender until creamy and smooth: cucumber, pineapple, frozen banana, light coconut milk, water, lime zest, lime juice, greens, and ice cubes.

2. For a thicker smoothie, add extra ice. For a thinner smoothie, add more of your preferred liquid. Taste the smoothie and adjust the flavors as needed by adding more lime juice or zest for acidity, more banana or pineapple for sweetness, more coconut milk for creaminess, or more greens for a deeper green color.

3 Once done, serve the smoothie. If you have any leftovers, they can be stored in the refrigerator for up to 24 hours.

Notes:

1. Try using canned light coconut milk. Alternatively, you can use coconut beverages from a carton or coconut water for a lighter smoothie.

2. You can also add some extra protein by including 1-2 tbsp of hemp seeds, chia seeds, or your preferred unflavored or vanilla-flavored protein powder. The Vega Viva Vanilla flavor is particularly pleasant, but you may have your own favorite brand or flavor.

CHAPTER 8
21-DAY MEAL PLAN

This is a sample menu for three weeks on the Mediterranean diet.

	DAY 1		DAY 2
Breakfast	Masala Omelet	Breakfast	Oatmeal Berry Breakfast Bake
Snack	4–5 Almonds	Snack	
Lunch	Zucchini Pasta with Lemon Garlic Shrimp	Lunch	Easy Chicken Gyros with Tzatziki Sauce
Dinner	Orange Glazed Salmon and Traditional Greek Salad	Dinner	Roasted Cabbage Steaks and Cherry Tomato and Asparagus Salad

	DAY 3		DAY 4
Breakfast	Easy Matcha Pancakes	Breakfast	Green Shakshuka
Snack	Pineapple Kale Smoothie	Snack	4–5 Almonds
Lunch	Greek Baked Zucchini and Potatoes	Lunch	Vegetarian Eggplant Moussaka
Dinner	Ratatouille	Dinner	Baked Tilapia Recipe With Pecan Rosemary Topping and Fig & Goat Cheese Salad

	DAY 5		DAY 6
Breakfast	Mediterranean Hummus Toast with Za'atar	Breakfast	Breakfast Protein Smoothie
Snack		Snack	Poached Eggs on Avocado & Feta Toast
Lunch	Coconut Shrimp Curry	Lunch	Traditional Spanish Paella; a Small Salad Of Choice
Dinner	Salmon with Lemony Asparagus and Carrots and 1 Serving Brown Rice	Dinner	Scallops with Lemon-Herb Sauce and Traditional Greek Salad

	DAY 7		DAY 8
Breakfast	Sweet Potato Fritters With Smashed Avocado	Breakfast	Amaranth Oatmeal
Snack	1 Portion of Fruit	Snack	White Bean Soup
Lunch	Mediterranean Turkey-Stuffed Peppers	Lunch	Fresh Mango Guacamole Recipe
Dinner	Shrimp Tacos	Dinner	Greek Chicken Kabobs and Tomato Peach Burrata Salad

	DAY 9		DAY 10
Breakfast	Salmon and Spinach Egg Muffins	Breakfast	Chia Pudding
Snack	1 Portion of Fruit	Snack	Beet, Grapefruit, and Feta Salad
Lunch	Traditional Greek Salad	Lunch	Basil Chicken with Kumquats
Dinner	Spicy Chicken and Sweet Potato Stew	Dinner	Baked Chicken and Ricotta Meatballs and 1 serving brown rice

	DAY 11		DAY 12
Breakfast	Vegan Banana pancakes	Breakfast	Green Smoothie
Snack	4–5 Almonds	Snack	Baked Blueberry & Banana-Nut Oatmeal Cups
Lunch	Veggistrone soup and Fig Salad With Parma ham & Blue Cheese	Lunch	Seared Tuna and Grilled Halloumi Salad
Dinner	Buffalo Chicken Zucchini Boats	Dinner	Arugula Salad with Pesto Shrimps, Parmesan and White Beans

	DAY 13		DAY 14
Breakfast	Spinach-Curry Crêpes	Breakfast	Shakshuka
Snack	No-Bake Rose Petal Brownies	Snack	Easy Thai Shrimp Soup
Lunch	Sweet Potato-Black Bean Burgers	Lunch	Low-Fat Turkey Bolognese
Dinner	Mixed Seafood Salad, a Large Portion	Dinner	Balsamic Roasted Vegetables

	DAY 15		DAY 16
Breakfast	Fig and Ricotta Toast	Breakfast	Blueberry Protein Shake
Snack	1 Portion of Fruit	Snack	Pineapple-Grapefruit Detox Smoothie
Lunch	Mediterranean Stuffed Peppers	Lunch	Homemade Chicken Gyros
Dinner	Mediterranean Baked Sweet Potatoes	Dinner	Cauliflower "Tabbouleh"

	DAY 17		DAY 18
Breakfast	Mediterranean Strata	Breakfast	Zucchini Fritters with Feta and Dill
Snack	Sweet Potato Black Bean Soup	Snack	4–5 Almonds
Lunch	Chicken Quinoa Bowl	Lunch	Balela Salad Recipe
Dinner	Stuffed Eggplant Recipe (Vegetarian)	Dinner	Anatolian Chicken Stew With Capers and Olives

	DAY 19		DAY 20
Breakfast	Greek Tuna Salad with Toast	Breakfast	Baba Ganoush
Snack	Strawberry Avocado Spinach Salad	Snack	Baked Pears
Lunch	Tofu Stir-Fry	Lunch	Creamy Tomato Risotto
Dinner	Mussels with Wine	Dinner	Instant Pot Harissa Bean Stew

	DAY 21
Breakfast	Cauliflower Fritters With Hummus
Snack	1 Portion of Fruit
Lunch	Baked Tilapia with Lemon
Dinner	Stuffed Grape Leaves

The Basic List Of Products That Should Always Be At Home:

THE BASIC LIST OF PRODUCTS

- Avocado
- Extra Virgin Olive Oil
- Lettuce
- Ramen
- Arugula
- Mangold
- Cabbage
- The Cruciferous Family
- Spinach
- Microgreens
- Calais
- Cilantro
- Basil
- Celery
- Asparagus
- Olives
- Zucchini
- Paprika
- Hummus
- Bean
- Broccoli
- Tomato
- Eggplant
- Onion
- Leek
- Shallot
- Beet

- Cauliflower
- Batata
- Chickpeas
- Porridge
- Brown Rice
- Amaranth
- Lentil
- Pea
- Whole Grain Oatmeal
- Buckwheat
- Bulgur
- Pearl Barley
- Quinoa
- Barley
- Pasta From Durum Wheat
- Aged Cheeses
- Feta
- MozzarKiwi
- All Berries
- All Kinds Of Nuts, Seeds
- ella
- Chicken
- Chicken Eggs
- Turkey
- Rabbit
- Salmon
- Tuna

- Mackerel
- Seabass Fish
- Telapia
- Dorado
- Swordfish
- Seafood
- Shrimp
- Sea Scallops
- Mussels
- Oysters
- Octopus
- Caviar
- Fruits
- Fig
- Garnet
- Grape
- Kiwi
- All Berries
- All Kinds Of Nuts, Seeds
- Pistachio
- Tonsil
- Walnut
- Hazelnut
- Seasonings
- Oregano
- Rosemary
- Thyme
- Turmeric
- Sage
- Cinnamon
- Cardamom
- Carnation
- Mint
- Fennel

Modern lifestyle and ecology affect us hugely. Old and new diseases occur, there is lack of the vital energy, stress, anxiety, etc. But we can change it by keeping ourselves healthier from within, especially by healthy eating and the Mediterranean Diet will help you in this!

Dear reader, I hope you find this book useful, and you are now a step closer to healthy living. I'd be very grateful for your comment.

Finally, please remember that the food you eat can be the most powerful form of medicine or the slowest form of poison. Take care!